Hans Küng and Reunion

G. H. DUGGAN, S.M.

THE NEWMAN PRESS
WESTMINSTER, MARYLAND

Contents

Introduction

There can be few educated Catholics in the English-speaking world who have not heard of Dr. Hans Küng, Professor of Fundamental Theology in the Faculty of Catholic Theology in the University of Tübingen. He made his mark in the theological world with a thesis on Karl Barth's theology of justification, but it is his books on the Ecumenical Council that have brought him to the notice of the general public.

The first of these, *The Council Reform and Reunion,* was published in 1961. Enthusiastically received by non-Catholics as well as Catholics, it ensured for the author large and sympathetic audiences in the United States and Britain when he undertook a lecture tour of these countries early in 1963. During 1963 he published two more books. The first, *That the World may Believe,* is a series of letters to young people on such topics as Catholic-Protestant relations, the Mass, the salvation of unbelievers, superstition and the difficulties of faith. The other, *The Council in Action*, bears the sub-title 'Reflections on the Second Vatican Council' and is a survey of the achievements of the first session and a programme for further developments.

During the Council he has been lecturing to groups of the Council Fathers, to students and the general public, and late in 1963 he appeared in a world-wide television broadcast as one of a panel of Catholic and Protestant speakers who discussed various religious and moral issues.

This book is an appraisal of Küng's thought as it is presented in the three works mentioned above. It is not concerned with the original German text, but with the English translations, through which his thought has had its impact on the English-speaking world. Hence it will not be a valid objection to adverse criticism of Küng – of which there will be plenty – to urge that what sounds badly in English is quite orthodox when read in the original German. Besides, since Küng reads and speaks English fluently, it is reasonable to suppose that he has inspected these translations.

Küng's praises have been sung so widely that there is little need to expatiate on what is valuable in his work. As a vigorous spokesman for the policy of 'aggiornamento' and ecumenical dialogue with our separated brethren, he has stimulated thought in Catholic circles about the many practical problems that confront us in our approach to the non-Catholic world. He has drawn attention to certain aspects of the Church's life that make the acceptance of her claims needlessly difficult, e.g. excessive centralization in government, the tendency to deny the need for reform within the Church, the use of Latin in the Liturgy. He has drawn a thought-provoking parallel between the Council convoked by men and the Church called together by God, and, in advocating a greater use of the vernacular in the liturgy and greater freedom of discussion in the Church, he has voiced sentiments that are shared by most members of the Council. He has also drawn the attention of Protestant theologians to some of the problems which they have to face, especially that presented by the New Testament witness to the existence of ecclesiastical authority in the Apostolic Church.

On the other hand his works abound in statements that are gravely misleading. It is not a question of such theological inexactitude or lack of balance as one might expect to find in books that are popular and occasional. Küng's shortcomings are of a different order. The misleading statement that is almost true, but not quite, seems to be his stock-in-trade. Here is a sample (f.a.q.) taken from the *Council Reform and Reunion:* 'At the time of the Reformation, the attack was directed not so much against devotion to Mary as against the exuberances of the cult of the saints in general' [1]. Now it is a commonplace that what the Reformers attacked was not exuberances in the cult of the saints, but the cult of the saints *tout court*. They regarded the cult of the saints, in any shape or form, as contrary to the basic Christian truth that there is only one mediator of God and men, the Man Christ Jesus.

This dangerous looseness of expression may be due to inexperience, for Küng is a comparatively young man – he is only thirty-five – and has not had time to make a thorough study of the manifold questions he discusses in these works. He ranges widely – through Church history, history of the liturgy, Scriptural exegesis, dogmatic and moral theology – and whatever may have been the case in the Middle Ages, it now takes many years of intensive study to arrive at true competence in any one of these fields of inquiry. Küng's unsatisfactory treatment of so much of what he handles may then be due to the fact that with much of it he can have only a superficial acquaintance.

A more likely explanation of his tendency to misstate and minimize the points on which Catholic and Protestant disagree is that he is moved by an injudicious zeal to win the Lutherans to corporate reunion. As we shall see, he misrepresents what Luther did at the Reformation and consistently plays down the dif-

---

1. *The Council, Reform and Reunion* (trans. by Cecily Hastings), New York: Sheed and Ward, 1961, p. 125. (To be quoted henceforward as CRR.)

ferences that now separate us from the Lutherans. In his account of the matter, Catholic and Lutheran are at one in holding the same faith; the differences are a matter of formulas. The Catholic formulas, like the Lutheran, are inadequate, and need to be amended in order to express the Gospel truth in its fullness. The Council of Trent slammed the door, behind the Protestants, defining the doctrines of the Church in terms of an antiquated unscriptural theology (e.g. 'transubstantiation'). It is the task of the Church in this century to correct these definitions, transposing the New Testament *kerygma* so as to put into the background what is unpalatable to the Protestants, and present the faith in scriptural terms which they will find acceptable. Küng does not express himself so bluntly, but this is the substance of his thought – what the average reader will gather from his works.

I write as a theologian, not primarily for theologians, but for the general public – priests, religious, layfolk – who have read Küng's works.

The book consists of three main parts. The first is historical and is a refutation of Küng's account of Luther's theological development. The second is doctrinal, being a criticism of Küng's views on the Church, considered in her structure, and her teaching authority and on the Holy Eucharist. The third deals with the subject of ecumenism.

'What the Church needs above all today', Küng writes, 'is honesty, the honesty to make a just assessment, without illusions... And secondly courage; the courage to say in season, out of season, what the situation demands... even at the grave risk of making oneself unpopular [1]. A sharp critique of the thought

---

1. *The Council in Action* (trans. by Cecily Hastings), New York: Sheed and Ward, 1963, p. 8 (To be quoted henceforward as CA.)

of Hans Küng is unlikely to prove a passport to popularity. As one of the Council Fathers wrote to me recently: 'It requires great courage to criticize these modern theologians. Those who have ventured to rebuke them are quickly the target of emotional attacks by the supporters of the avant-garde'. The outlook, it appears, is stormy.

CHAPTER 1

The Theological Development of Martin Luther

Luther, as portrayed by Küng, was an ardent soul burning with zeal for the reform of the Church and unfortunate enough to be living in an age when the concrete situation of the Papacy made it impossible to see the nature of the Papacy clearly. Finding that no attempt was being made by the rulers of the Church to meet his legitimate demands for reform, and perhaps discouraged by the failure of the Fifth Lateran Council to achieve the reforms that were its avowed objective, he gradually came to adopt an untenable position on the subject of justification. His central demand was for reform of the Church in head and members, and his doctrine of justification was only a lever, a stick to beat the Papacy with. Formulating this doctrine in terms which the Church could not then accept, he refused to give it up when called upon by the Pope to do so and went into schism. This schism was a reaction against an over-authoritarian, centralist, and uniformist conception on the part of the Latin Church, which was more or less suppressing the Church's original pluralism. Thus, by its lack of tact and understanding, the Roman Church is co-responsible for the schism that has divided Western Christendom these last four hundred years [1].

The story of Luther as Küng tells it is, let it be said at once, a fairy tale from the Tübingen woods. The tragic hero, forced into heresy against his will by the incapacity of the Church's leaders to understand the spiritual needs of the age in all their pro-

1. Cf. CA. pp. 28, 32, 222; CRR. 130, 184.

fundity is a creature of Küng's imagination. The Luther of history is a different person altogether.

Take Küng's contention that the Lutheran Reformation was primarily a matter of practical reform. He writes: 'It was the requirements of reform at the practical, concrete level, and not simply abstract theological propositions that fired the Reformation' [1]. What fired the Reformation was Luther's revolutionary conception of the Christian faith, and this was not a set of abstract theological propositions but the message that salvation is through faith in Christ, good works being quite unnecessary. It suffices to read Luther's tract *Concerning Christian Liberty* to understand the immense appeal of Lutheranism to a world in which, largely through lack of instruction, faith had degenerated into formalism.

Luther, the knight in shining armour, anxious to put his sword at the service of the Church, and compelled by circumstances to turn against her, is the tragic hero in the following story of the Reformation: 'All the same, Church reform collapsed in the later Middle Ages, in spite of the efforts of several Councils. In many ways, it was a very bad time in the Catholic Church. This led to Luther's great protest, and this in turn to his rebellion against the Catholic Church as she existed then, and to his expulsion from our Church. What Luther wanted was good in itself: he wanted the Church to frame herself and her theology anew according to the Gospel of Christ, to renew and reform herself. But there were other, less good, factors at work along with these good demands; and not least, politics. And so, for the sake of Church reform, there came the tragedy of schism, which, as you know, has lasted until the present day. The Catholic Church could not accept Luther's way of Church re-

1. CRR. p. 102.

form for various reasons which I do not need to explain here; in that time of crisis Luther abandoned many things which must not be abandoned if one is really going to keep to the Scriptures' [1].

What can we say of this travesty of Reformation history? What Luther wanted was that the Church should adopt an entirely novel interpretation of the Christian faith. The Gospel of Christ according to which he wanted her to 'frame herself and her theology anew' was the Gospel as interpreted by Martin Luther. Whether or not this was 'good in itself' is a theological question, which the Church, then as now, has always answered in the negative. When Luther was informed that his new version of the faith was contrary to the teaching of the Church, he refused to retract, and as Küng admits elsewhere, it was this, rather than his departure from the teaching of Scripture that made him a heretic [2].

Luther, the practical reformer, who is gradually forced into heresy because his zeal for reform was thwarted by selfseeking prelates – how did Küng come to form this completely fanciful picture of the great Reformer? I suspect that he relies heavily on Lortz's work *Die Reformation in Deutschland* which he describes as 'the standard Catholic work today' [3] and 'an epoch-making work which has established itself plainly in the face of all its predecessors' [4]. Now Lortz's book belongs to the genre of historical interpretation rather than to the category of books which tell a complete story, and quite apart from the fact that some historians do not accept Lortz's inter-

1. *That the World May Believe* (trans. by Cecily Hastings), New York: Sheed and Ward, 1963, p. 42. (To be quoted henceforward as WB.)
2. CRR. p. 74.
3. CRR. p. 146.
4. CRR. p. 104.

pretation of history, it is plain that a work of this kind can never supersede the straightforward histories of such writers as Grisar. And when we read straightforward history, we find that the facts, about which there is no dispute, make nonsense of Küng's 'history'.

Nurtured in the Nominalist theology then dominant in the intellectual circles in which he moved, Luther was preoccupied with the question of his personal holiness and predestination. He wanted to be absolutely certain that he was pleasing to God and that his name was written in the Book of Life. At the same time he was keenly aware of the deeply rooted tendencies to sin within his own heart. The problem was to reconcile this awareness of sin with the certainty of enjoying the favour of God, and he solved it with his theory of justification by faith alone. For Luther, justification consists in this, that man, while remaining plunged in sin, ceases to have his sin imputed to him because of his faith. Faith is confidence that one is saved through the merits of Christ, which are, as it were, a cloak covering one's sinfulness. So long as a man clings to this certainty that Christ has died to atone for *his* sins, his salvation is assured. Whether he behaves well or ill does not affect the issue.

When did Luther arrive at this notion of justification? Quite certainly he had it long before he clashed with the Pope. Hirsch maintains that he held this doctrine *in nuce* as early as 1509. Brandenburg finds many of the elements of the theory in his *Commentary of the Psalms* delivered in the university 1513-1515, but Denifle considers that in this work his doctrine is still orthodox.

Luther himself indicates a date early in 1513 as the moment of the great revelation. He was, he tells us in the tower (more exactly, the 'cloaca') of the monastery, when he received from the Holy Spirit this flash of light which resolved all his uncertainties and filled his soul with a deep and abiding peace. Till the end of his life he regarded himself as having received a special mission from God to preach the doctrine which had brought him such consolation and exhilaration of spirit, and he felt the more reassured because he had received from the Church a doctorate in divinity, which he regarded as a commission to teach.

It took some time for Luther to see all the implications of his tremendous intuition, but already in his *Commentary on the Romans,* delivered in the university between April 1515 and October 1516, his doctrine is fully heretical, as the following quotation will show. He writes: 'For if the confessions of the saints are to be understood only with respect to their past sins, and they show themselves pure in the present, why, then, do they confess not only their past sins but also their present sins? It is only because they know that sin is in them but that it is covered and not counted because of Christ, and because they want to testify that all their good is outside themselves in Christ, who nonetheless is in them through faith ... Because of the fact that we cannot fulfil the commandments of God and thus are always deservedly unrighteous, there is nothing left to us but that we ever fear the judgement and pray for the remission of unrighteousness, or rather, for its non-imputation' [1].

He defended this theory in theological disputations at Wittenberg in 1516 and 1517, and at Heidelberg in 1518. By 1520 he had worked out some of its principal implications, e.g. that good works are not necessary for salvation, the Mass is not a sacrifice, there

1. *Lectures on Romans* (Tr. W. Pauck), SCM Press, London, 1961, pp. 134, 144.

is no essential difference between priest and layman, the rule of faith is Holy Scripture interpreted by the individual Christian.

As John Eck had already perceived in 1518, and as was clear to everyone by 1520, Lutheranism was a very radical kind of heresy. It was as Küng admits, 'essentially a revolution' [1]. This being so, it is difficult to understand why Küng consistently refers to the Lutheran revolt and its consequences as 'schism' [2]. What justification can there be, for example, for a statement such as the following: 'The eastern schism has been going on for over 900 years, the northern one for over 400. 900 years and 400 years of schism cannot be simply uprooted by a conference' [3]? As every theologian – indeed, every well-informed person – knows, there is a world of difference between the schism of the Orthodox and the heresy of Luther, and it is a serious abuse of language to use the one therm for both. Philip Hughes has been at pains to show that 'schism' is used erroneously to designate Henry VIII's breach with Rome, but one can understand how men came to speak of the Henrician 'schism', for Anglican doctrine under Henry bore a marked resamblance to the Catholic faith. Lutheranism from the first was obviously a horse of a different colour – a heresy if ever there was one.

It is not as if Küng had unwittingly overlooked the difference between heresy and schism, for he refers to it explicitly. He writes: '*Hairesis* (Greek for 'heresy') is clearly distinguished from *schisma*, and indicates a further stage beyond it. This difference in degree consists in the fact that *hairesis* strikes at the

1. CRR. p. 74.
2. CRR. pp. 72, 74, 86, 95, 151, 159, 184; WB. 16, 19, 20, 42, 77, 81, 83; CA. 20, 42, 77, 81, 83; CA. 20, 21, 23, 26, 32, 247, 258, 267.
3. CA. p. 20.

foundation of the Church, which is doctrine'[1]. One cannot then but wonder why he speaks of Lutheranism as 'schism' when he should be calling it 'heresy'. In the interests of ecumenical charity we refrain from speaking of our contemporaries as 'heretics' or 'schismatics', but that is no reason why systems of thought should be given misleading labels. In ecumenical dialogue, as elsewhere, honesty is surely the best policy.

It is possible that Küng doubts whether Luther's doctrine of justification is fundamentally heretical, for he writes: 'The article of faith which was once regarded as the theological root of the schism of the Reformation, but which could scarcely serve to bring about any division from the Church whatsoever: the doctrine of the justification of the sinner by God's grace'[2].

If this refers to Luther's doctrine of justification, it implies that at the Council of Trent the Church was shadow-sparring. Her carefully formulated anathemas would have been directed, not against Luther's doctrine but a figment of her imagination. And this would imply that we in the twentieth century are better acquainted with the facts of the situation than the men on the spot – an hypothesis which the historian will find very dubious and the theologian quite untenable.

If Küng is referring to the doctrine of justification as we find it in the works of the modern Lutherans like Barth, the statement is still erroneous, for their teaching differs widely from the official teaching of the Church as defined at the Council of Trent. For the modern Lutherans, as for Luther, grace is not an intrinsic elevation of man's being but God's favour freely imputed to the elect, nor does the adult actively

1. CA. pp. 192–193, note.
2. CRR. p. 116.

cooperate by charity in the work of justification itself.

There are grounds for thinking that Küng's failure to perceive the gulf that lies between the Catholic account of justification and the Lutheran may be due to the inadequacy of his own concept of justification. He writes: 'It is God's grace that alone justifies sinful man. But he who is justified by God's grace has to prove his faith by works of love ... In the cross and resurrection of Christ God has shown himself gracious towards all men, adjudging them righteous. A man has to abandon himself to God empty-handed, without works, putting his whole trust in him; in short he has to believe. It is only from this state that he can then fruitfully do the works of love' [1].

It will not be easy to reconcile this account of justification, with its distinctly Lutheran overtones, with the teaching of the Church, defined at Trent, that charity is not merely the consequence of the process of justification but is one of its constituent elements.

Here are the relevant canons:

'If anyone shall say that men are justified by the mere imputation of the justice of Christ or by the remission of their sins, excluding grace and charity which is diffused in their hearts by the Holy Spirit and inheres in them, or that the grace by which we are justified is merely the favour of God, let him be anathema.

'If anyone shall say that justifying faith is nothing else than trust in the divine mercy remitting sins on account of Christ, or that this trust is that alone by which we are justified, let him be anathema'.

Küng's account of justifying faith is expressed quite briefly and it may be possible to reconcile his thought

---

1. *Eucharist Sacrifice and the Reformation* by F. Clark, S.J. (Westminster, Md.: The Newman Press, 1961), p. 106.

with the teaching of Trent; but he seems to have gone out of his way to clothe his thought in language which the Council anathematized, identifying 'faith' with trust in the mercy of God. I invite the reader to compare Küng's description with the account of faith which the Council condemned in the second of the canons I have quoted above.

Luther and Papal Authority

Quite early in his career as an heresiarch Luther rejected the authority of the Pope. In the 95 Theses of 1517 he denied that the Pope has any real juridical authority. As one writer puts it, he reduced the Pope to the level of a Protestant pastor. In 1519 he had begun to speak of the Pope as Antichrist, and in his *Babylonian Captivity,* published in October 1520, he further developed this idea, which remained one of the axioms of his ecclesiology to the end. As time went on, his hatred of the Papacy became almost pathological, reaching the climax of its expression in the *Abbildung des Papsttums* a series of scurrilous woodcuts, which he published in 1545 [1].

What was the reason for Luther's rejection of Papal authority? Was it the low moral character of such Renaissance Popes as Alexander VI? This seems to be Küng's view, for he writes: 'Luther's denial of the Petrine office (for which his theology prepared the way, but which it did not make inevitable) did not fundamentally have a theoretical, exegetical or historical basis but was due to practical, existential forces at work in the situation at that time. Luther's opposition to the Pope did not begin from some new interpretation of Matt. 16.18 or John 21; the new exegetical and historical interpretation was a *consequence* of Luther's opposition to the Pope; and the

1. Cf. Denifle, Luther et le Lutheranisme (tr. J. Paquier), Paris, 2nd. Edn, 1914, Vol. IV, appendix II.

opposition itself has to be explained in terms of the situation of Luther, of the Church at that time, and the politics of that time, especially by the obscuring of the idea of the primacy by abuses in the Curia and by the Conciliar Movement. The *concrete* situation of the Papacy at that time made it impossible to see the *nature* of the Papacy clearly – and this is why the Papacy was denied' [1]. And elsewhere, in similiar vein: 'The *concrete existential situation* of the Petrine office *then,* in the age of the Renaissance, made it impossible to see clearly the true nature of the Petrine office' [2].

This explanation of Luther's denial of the Papal claims is shot through with sophistry. Küng argues that because Luther did not start from the Gospel texts that refer to the primacy, therefore his denial of the Petrine office did not have a theoretical exegetical basis. Can he be so ill acquainted with Luther's thought as not to know that Luther's denial of the Petrine office has *another* theoretical and exegetical basis, namely, his interpretation of the text that man is justified by faith, or, as Luther put it, by 'faith alone'? And if the concrete situation of the Papacy in that age made it *impossible* to see clearly the nature of the Papal office, how is it that so many Catholic writers, like Alveld, Cajetan, Fisher, sprang to the defence of the Papacy when Luther attacked it? If Küng, when he wrote 'impossible' meant 'rather difficult', why could he not have written 'rather difficult'? Extravagant statements come ill from a trained theologian, even in works intended for the general public.

The truth of the matter is that Luther's rejection of Papal authority was not due to any difficulty he may have experienced in reconciling the claims made for the Petrine office with the character of the men who

1. CRR. p. 133.
2. CA. p. 223.

occupied the Papal throne in his time, nor to any confusion caused by the Conciliar Movement. His objections went much deeper and sprang, not from the concrete existential situation of his time, but from his theological principles. Luther saw quite early that his theory of justification by faith alone implied a denial of any divinely appointed hierarchy in the Church. Already in 1518 he had accepted the Hussite doctrine that the true Church, the Church of the promises and the Mystical Body of Christ is invisible. Luther's saving faith is the response of the individual soul to the Word of God revealed in Scripture; in his theology there is no place for any created activity to mediate to men God's saving action nor for any active sharing by men in the dispensation of grace or divine truth. Pope or bishop have no more doctrinal authority than any other Christian. So we find Luther writing in 1520 that 'it may come to pass that the Pope and his followers are wicked and not true Christians, and not being taught by God, have no true understanding (of the Scriptures), whereas a common man may have true understanding' [1].

Luther and the Hierarchy

In the face of the plain facts of history, Küng maintains that Luther had no objection to episcopacy. He writes: 'Luther wanted to reform and renew the old Church. He took for granted ecclesiastical office, and the episcopal office in particular; he did not want to destroy it, but to reform it according to the Gospel. But to a large extent the worldly men who were in office set themselves against all reform of the Church and of their offices, for which they are gravely to blame. This meant that Luther, and the Reformers in general, fell into a tragic conflict with office as it existed

---

1. *Concerning Christian Liberty* in *Luther's Primary Works* (Ed. Wace, H. and Bucheim London 1896 p. 170).

in the Church, with the episcopal office and especially with the Petrine office' [1].

Here once again we have Luther cast in the role of the zealous reformer, anxious only to renew the Church according to the Gospel but thwarted by self-seeking prelates and forced into heresy.

What are the facts? In the first place, it is not at all certain that Luther thought of himself as a reformer. In the *Preface* written in 1545, eleven months before he died, he summed up his life in its various stages. In this balance sheet the word 'reform' does not appear; his only aim, he says, was to return to the sources of the faith – the Bible and the Fathers. However that may be, it is certain that Luther's 'reform' of the episcopacy amounted to a complete rejection of episcopacy as an institution enjoying any warrant in Scripture. He denied in the plainest language that there is any divinely instituted hierarchy in the Church. In 1520 he wrote: 'Let every man recognise what he is, and be certain that we are all equally priests, that is, we have the same power in the word and in any sacrament whatever' [2].

Küng is therefore guilty of a serious equivocation when he uses the same phrase to designate the Lutheran and the Catholic doctrines of the priesthood of all believers, as he does on page 81 of *The Council in Action*. There we read that Luther brings into play 'one of his fundamental insights into the nature of the Church, the universal priesthood of all believers' and a little later that 'the doctrine of the universal priesthood is one of the fundamental truths of Catholic ecclesiology'. Need we remark that for Luther 'the universal priesthood of all believers' means that every believer is his own priest and bishop and has no

1. CA. p. 222.
2. *Babylonian Captivity* in *Luther's Primary Works*, p. 396.

need of any other? Or that the Catholic doctrine is quite different?

Luther and the Mass

Küng has not a great deal to say about Luther's teaching on the Mass, but he manages to convey the impression that Luther was mainly concerned to root out abuses that had crept in during the later Middle Ages and to restore the Eucharistic liturgy to its original simplicity.

Why did Luther and the other Reformers leave the Church? One reason, says Küng, is their zeal for a more perfect liturgy. They wanted to have a genuine service of thanksgiving instead of the Mass and this was impossible if they remained in the Church. He writes: 'The Orthodox, the Lutherans, the Anglicans, the Free Churches did not separate themselves from us out of mere ill-will but because (allowing for the very many different factors which play their part in a schism) they considered that there were certain good and necessary things for which there was no room, no understanding in the Catholic Church. The Reformers, for instance, wanted to have a liturgy which would be once more a genuine service of thanksgiving for everything that Christ has done for us; not a Mass whispered by a priest to himself in a foreign language . . . [1].

This picture of Luther, Zwingli, Calvin, Bucer, Bullinger, Cranmer and the rest of them as liturgical idealists, compelled by their idealism to leave the Church, is pure fantasy. However much they differed among themselves in their teaching on the Eucharist, these men were at one in their detestation of any sacrificial interpretation of the Lord's Supper, and in devising their various liturgies their main preoccupation

---

1. WB. p. 83. Note the vague parenthesis, which may serve as an escape-clause.

was to exclude anything that might suggest to their followers that the ceremony in which they were taking part was in any sense a sacrificial offering of the Body and Blood of Christ.

What led Luther to repudiate the Mass was not the language in which it was celebrated, nor the rites developed by the Church in the course of ages, nor any of the abuses that had crept in during the Middle Ages. His attitude was based on something much more substantial. Quite simply, there was no place in Luther's new theology for the offering of a sacrifice like the Mass. Already in his *Commentary on the Hebrews* in 1517 he was emphasizing that Christ's sacrifice is in the past and presenting the Mass as a testament reminding us of the oblation once made. He had begun to attack the Mass directly in 1519 and in the *Babylonian Captivity* we find him explicitly denying that Christ offered a sacrifice at the Supper and describing the Mass as a 'scandal' and an 'impious abuse'. The Eucharist, he says, is simply an outward sign in which we are promised justification through faith.

'Luther's cardinal objection against the traditional doctrine of the Mass', Clark writes, 'was that it was a "work", something which belonged to that whole order of mediation, of man's active participation in the economy of grace that was anathema to the Reformer' [1].

Küng's picture of Luther leaving the Church in search of a vernacular liturgy is an example of the well-known error of reading history backwards. Finding himself in heresy with a host of followers, Luther had to provide them with a liturgy that would be in accord with the new beliefs. His first *Formula Missae,* published in 1523, was in Latin. This may have been a concession to the neophytes. More probably, he had

1. *Eucharistic Sacrifice and the Reformation,* Darton, Longman, and Todd, London, 1960, p. 106.

not yet realized the propagandist value of a German liturgy. His first effort in this direction is the *Deutsche Messe und Ordnungs Gottesdienst,* which appeared in 1526.

Curiously enough in this German Mass there is no offertory and no preface. Since it is in the preface that explicit mention is made of our duty of thanksgiving, Luther's German Mass hardly merits the description of 'a service of thanksgiving'. So much for Küng's statement that 'the Reformers wanted to have a liturgy that would once more be a genuine service of thanksgiving' [1].

---

1. Cf. B. Peauchmaurd, art. *La Messe est-elle pour Luther une action de grâces?* in Revue des Sc. Phil. et Théol., 1959, pp. 632–642.

CHAPTER 2

The Theology of Hans Küng

1. THE CHURCH

We have now to deal with the theology of Küng himself in so far as it can be ascertained from the books we are discussing. We shall concern ourselves with the two theological topics of which he mainly treats – the Church and the Mass.

In the Church we have first to consider her structure and holiness, with particular attention to the Papacy. Then we pass to a consideration of her teaching authority, dealing with such topics as her relation to Holy Scripture, the nature of dogmatic definitions, and the function of theology.

The Juridical Structure of the Church

As the kingdom of God on earth and the Mystical Body of Christ, the Church has a twofold nature. On the one hand she is a visible society, a corporate entity existing and acting in the world of men, the Catholic Church, with which for two millenniums the rulers of states have had to deal and whose history is so large a part of the history of Europe. On the other hand she is an object of faith, the Bride of Christ, who brings forth her children and nurtures them with the Word of God and the sacraments so as to prepare them for eternal life.

In a well-balanced theological account of the Church due attention will be paid to both these elements:

her juridical structure and her interior life of union with God. Both are essential, for God has ordained that man is to be sanctified as a member of a society that is at once human and divine, and no society can subsist without a juridical structure, any more than an organism could survive if it were only a blob of undifferentiated protoplasm.

When we say that the Church has a juridical structure, we mean that it is a true society, in which certain persons exercise authority and others are subject to authority, so that on the one hand there is a moral right to command and on the other a moral obligation to obey, and with the moral right to command the right to employ sanctions in case of disobedience.

It is Catholic teaching that the juridical structure of the Church is supernatural, being of divine institution and ordained to supernatural ends; but it pertains to the Church only as existing in this world, and is subordinated as a means to ends that are eternal and of an essentially higher order than itself.

It is true that since the Reformation Catholic theologians, in reacting against the Protestant notion of an invisible Church, have tended to over-emphasise the juridical aspect of the Church, as if this were the most important thing about her. In our own time certain theologians, and Küng is one of them, have shown a tendency to go to the opposite extreme.

Take, for example, this passage in which Küng contrasts the juridical and the spiritual conceptions of apostolic succession: In the Catholic Church efforts have been and are being made .... at a theological explanation of the apostolic succession – not in an external sense (as though the conferring of office by ordination were an almost automatic mechanism) but in a spiritualized sense (the apostolic succession as the outward sign, presupposing faith, of the free activity of the Holy Spirit, who is the source of all gifts and powers). The Scripture significantly uses for ecclesiastical office not the words *arche* and *exousia* ('office' in the sense of 'power'), which were current in the secular domain, but *diakonia* ('service'). Ecclesiastical office is now being seen primarily not so much as authority but rather as service; service of the Gospel, to the measure and pattern of the Gospel; and so not as an autonomous institution but one bound to the risen Lord and his Holy Spirit for the benefit and blessing of the faithful' [1].

Küng's thought here is not very clear, but he seems to be guilty of a false antithesis, as if the external (juridical) and spiritual aspects of apostolic succession were mutually exclusive, whereas in fact they are complementary. Ecclesiastical office involves a call to service, but it also confers true authority. Christ our Lord, who said 'I am in the midst of you as he that serveth', also said 'You call me Master and Lord, and you say well, for so I am'. Similarly, the Apostles and their successors, who carry on his work, receive from Him the commission to serve in the building up of the Church, and the juridical authority without which that task would be impossible.

We find the same false antithesis between juridical and spiritual in another passage where Küng declares that Catholic theology today 'sees the succession of apostolic office not as an automatic transmission of office through ordination but as the outward sign of the free action of the Spirit' [2]. The section in which this appears provides an interesting example of his dialectical method. First, he points out how the ecumenical council 'raises the problem which is cen-

1. CRR. pp. 130–131.
2. CA. p. 61.

tral to the Catholic-Protestant dialogue today; the problem of ecclesiastical office and its function'. Then he says: 'I am not here dealing with the problem of office', and concludes: 'Catholic theology today cannot fail to press Protestant theology for an answer on what it believes concerning the succession not only of apostolic belief and confession of faith, but also of the special apostolic office for the preservation of that belief and confession of faith'. If he is not dealing with the problem of office, one wonders what he is dealing with.

Küng's own solution of the problem naturally rules out the idea that the bishops are merely delegates of their communities, but it seems to imply that the hierarchy is subordinate to Holy Scripture, a point on which we shall have more to say later.

On this matter of the relation between the juridical and the spiritual in the structure of the Church Küng's thought is elusive, but I think it is pertinent in this context to recall a warning issued by the present Pope when Archbishop of Milan: 'To speak of the spiritual as opposed to the juridical Church is extremely dangerous, because it lends authority to concepts that are only approximate and imprecise, encourages hankerings after subversion, and fosters false hopes [1].

Holy Scripture and the Protestant Conception of the Church

Küng seems to hold that the New Testament contains contradictory conceptions of the Church, charismatic on the one hand and hierarchical on the other. Thus there would be Scriptural warrant for the Protestant views no less than for the Catholic. This divergence

1. Cf. *The Advocate*, Melbourne, Oct. 3, 1963, p. 26.

in the witness of Scripture to the Church would be only a particular instance exemplifying the general principle that changing situations and individuals were bound to give rise to divergences, amounting to opposition, in the Gospel record.

He writes: 'As the situation in which the proclamation was made kept changing, it compelled a constant modification of the original message, and the human and theological individuality of each new person making the proclamation played a considerable role in this. Hence mutually opposed differences in the New Testament were bound to come about, just as, significantly, what the tradition gives us is not *one* Gospel nor a Gospel-harmony nor any "life of Jesus", but different and often mutually opposed Gospels' [1].

If we once admit that there is mutual opposition between the Gospels, we shall find little difficulty in admitting that the New Testament contains opposed ecclesiological statements, some of which provide a basis for the Catholic view of the Church and others for a Lutheran one. This seems to be Küng's position, for he admits that the multiplicity of Christian confessions is to be accounted for by divergences in the New Testament record. He writes: 'The Canon of the New Testament does lie at the root of there being a multiplicity of confessions. We must grant Käsemann this point: for (a) the variety of Christian confessions is something that exists; (b) the various confessions do appeal to the Canon of the New Testament and refer themselves to it; (c) these various appeals have a *fundamentum in re,* being founded on the complexity already described. To this extent, then, the Canon of the New Testament lies at the root of the multiplicity

1. CA. p. 186.

of confessions' [1].

Surely Küng is here granting Käsemann more than Catholic theology will allow. On these principles, one would have to admit that Arianism, Christian Science, and Mormonism have an objective basis in Scripture, for all have really existed, and all appeal to the New Testament as warrant for their beliefs.

The Holiness of the Church

For Luther, a human being even after justification always remains a sinner, not merely in the sense that he retains tendencies to sin, but is guilty of actual sin. Human nature has been so corrupted by original sin that it is incapable of any good, and what we commonly regard as our good deeds are really sins. However, faith in Christ's word ensures that these sins are no longer imputed to us. Thus we are just through our faith in Christ and unjust because of our ineradicable inherent sinfulness. As Luther put it: God is wonderful in His saints; to Him they are at the same time just and unjust' [2].

In the same way, the Church, which is composed of these sinful human beings, is at once holy and sinful – holy because of the faith that causes sin to be no longer imputed, sinful because it is composed of sinners who ever remain steeped in sin.

I think it is fair to say that Küng's account of the Church has been coloured by this Lutheran pessimism, for though he stresses the holiness of Christ, and of her doctrine and the means of grace, he suggests that for the bulk of Christians these remain ineffectual. He writes: 'As coming from God the Church is and

1. CA. p. 171–172.
2. Quoted in Denifle, op. cit. Vol. II, p. 447.

remains holy, she is holy not through the spirit of her sinful members, but through Christ's doctrine and sacraments' [1].

In the same context he quotes a passage from Karl Rahner in which Rahner, after arbitrarily excluding from his consideration the saints –'perhaps many such' – who are found in the Church, says: 'The Church is a sinful Church: that is a truth of faith.' Far from being a truth of faith, this statement of Rahner's is quite erroneous. Küng does not accept it, preferring the expression 'the Church of sinners'. But this expression, too, smacks of Lutheranism and should be discarded. St. Paul had no compunction about addressing the faithful as 'saints'. It might not be a bad idea, if our modern theologians, who are so insistent that their theology is scriptural, took a leaf out of the Apostle's book.

The Papacy

The primacy and infallibility of the Roman Pontiff is one of the great stumbling-blocks in the way of reunion. As Archbishop Davidson said at the time of the Malines Conversations: 'Prior to all these (other questions) and far outweighing them in importance, stands the fundamental question – Is there, or is there not, a Vicar of Christ upon earth, who possesses *iure divino* a authoritative position in relation to the whole of Christendom?' [2].

Given the importance of this issue and the need for complete frankness towards our separated brethren,

1. CRR. p. 31.
2. Quoted by D. L. Greenstock in art. *Unity: Special Problems, Dogmatic and Moral* in *The Thomist*, Oct. 1963, Vol. XXVII, p. 610.

it is disquieting to find that Küng plays down the role of the Papacy in the life of the Church. He writes: 'I shall suggest ... that the whole of our terminology about the primacy needs overhauling in the light of Scripture. In terms of Holy Scripture, it is anything but natural and obvious that the Pope should, for instance, be called "Head" of the Church. In the New Testament, this term is reserved to Christ, while Peter is called the "foundation", etc. Is not one perhaps doing an outright disservice to the papal primacy by transferring Christological terms to the Pope?' [1].

Küng is seriously mistaken here. The root of his error is the principle – a principle that vitiates so much of his theology – that the theologian's starting-point is Holy Scripture. This may be true of the Protestant theologian; it is not true of the Catholic, who starts from Tradition. As Weigel says: 'Tradition is the basis of the theologian's investigation. Where will he find it? First of all, in the historical statements of the total episcopate. This means the doctrine of all ecumenical councils. The Catholic theologian will also include under such statements *ex cathedra* definitions of the Papacy ... [2].

That the Pope should be called the 'Head of the Church' is taught by Catholic tradition in the plainest terms. We have, for instance, the decree of the Council of Florence: 'We define that the holy Apostolic See and the Roman Pontiff holds the primacy over the whole world, and that the Roman Pontiff himself is the successor of blessed Peter, the Prince of the Apostles, and the true Vicar of Christ, and is Head of the whole Church and the Father and Teacher of all Christians ... [3].

1. CA. pp. 230–231.
2. *Where Do We Differ?*, Burns Oates, London, 1962, p. 93.
3. Cf. Denzinger, *Enchiridion Symbolorum*, n. 694.

This definition of the year 1439 made the position of the Papacy quite plain for any Catholic well before Luther's time.

Catholic doctrine on the point was defined even more precisely at the Vatican Council. The canons read:

'If anyone shall say that blessed Peter the Apostle was not constituted by Christ the Lord as Prince of all the Apostles and Visible Head of the whole Church Militant, or that he received directly and immediately from the same Jesus Christ our Lord a primacy of honour only and not of jurisdiction in the true and proper sense, let him be anathema'.

'If anyone shall say that it was not by the institution of Christ the Lord Himself i.e. *iure divino,* that blessed Peter should have an unending line of successors in the primacy over the whole Church, or that the Roman Pontiff is not the blessed Peter's successor in the same primacy, let him be anathema' [1].

In the face of these solemn definitions of the Church, it is surely temerarious to speak of 'the need for overhauling the whole of our terminology about the primacy in the light of Scripture'. If, using the language of the First Vatican Council, we speak of the Pope as the successor of St. Peter and therefore 'the Visible Head of the Church Militant', this may jar on the ears of our separated brethren. But the Catholic theologian can do no other. It is not for him to water down the solemn definitions of ecumenical councils in order to bring them into harmony with his, or other people's, interpretation of the New Testament.

Catholic tradition on the subject was summed up by St. Thomas when he answered the question: 'Whether to be Head of the Church is proper to Christ?' At first glance it might seem that he favours Küng's view,

1. Denzinger, op. cit. nn. 1823, 1825.

for he writes: 'It is written (Col 2, 19): 'The head of the Church is that from which the whole body by joints and bands being supplied with nourishment and compacted, groweth in the increase of God''. But this belongs only to Christ. Therefore Christ alone is head of the Church'.

However, in the body of the article, he explains that although Christ alone is Head as being the source of grace and justification, the term 'head' may be applied by analogy to others. He writes: 'Others, who exercise exterior guidance over the Church, may be called heads of the Church; differently, however, from Christ. First, inasmuch as Christ is the Head of all who pertain to the Church in every time and place and state; but all other men are called heads with reference to certain special places, as bishops of their churches; or with reference to a determined time – the Pope is head of the whole Church – viz. during the time of his Pontificate – and with reference to a determined state, inasmuch as they are in the state of wayfarers. Secondly, because Christ is the Head of the Church by his own power and authority, and others are called heads, as taking Christ's place...' [1].

Turning next to Holy Scripture, we find that the teaching of Tradition, summed up by St. Thomas and authoritatively formulated by the Councils of Florence and First Vatican, is, as we might have expected, in full accord with the teaching of the New Testament. It is true that in the Epistles of St. Paul, the term 'Head of the Church' is applied exclusively to Christ, but just because Luther confined his attention to St. Paul, that is no reason why we should do so. When we turn to the Gospels, we find cogent grounds for affirming that St. Peter was appointed by Christ to be his Vicar on earth, the Visible Head of the Church

1. *Summa Theologica,* III. q. 8. a. 3.

Militant. There is, in fact, a curious parallelism between several features which we should have been inclined to think were the exclusive property of Christ.

Let us glance briefly at some of the texts. First we have Matthew 16, where Christ, the stone which the builders rejected (Matt. 21), declares that Peter is the Rock on which he will build his Church. Küng misses the point of this metaphor, for he takes it to signify that St. Peter, together with the other Apostles is the foundation on which the Church is built, as if 'rock' and 'foundation' are interchangeable terms. Thus, speaking of the Petrine office, he says that 'what was once *laid* as a foundation would continue to *function* as a foundation' [1], and more explicitly: 'It was not to Peter alone but to the whole apostolic college that Christ entrusted his Church, just as it is not only Peter but (somthing often overlooked) the Apostles as well who are the foundation, the rock of the Church (Eph. 2, 20; Apoc. 21, 14). It is not to the Pope alone but to the whole episcopal college that Christ has entrusted his Church' [2].

What Küng has failed to remark is that the rock is not the foundation of a building, but that on which the foundations rest. It is clear from the Gospel that it is Peter, and Peter alone, who is the rock, as his name indicates. It was Simon, and Simon only, who had his name changed to Peter. On this Rock, the bedrock, the foundations of the Church – the other Apostles – are laid. As a wise builder, Christ built not on sand but on rock, and the rock is Peter: Thou art Peter, and on this rock I will build my Church.

Similarly, it is prophesied of the Messias (Is. 22. 22) that he will be the bearer of the keys i.e. he will possess the fullness of authority in the kingdom of God.

1. CRR. p. 140.
2. CA. p. 241.

Christ uses the same image when he promises that Peter will take his place: 'To *thee* will I give the keys of the kingdom of heaven'.

St. Matthew (c. 17) records an incident in which Clement of Alexandria already saw a clear testimony to Peter's unique role as head of the Church. When the Temple officials came to collect the half-stater, a tax payable by the head of every household, Christ bade Peter catch a fish and give them the coin he would find in its mouth. Now this coin was a stater, sufficient to pay the tax twice over. 'Give that to them', Christ said, 'for me and for *thee*'. This surely implies that the Apostolic group, has two heads – Christ and Peter. Or rather, Christ is the head of the household now, and Peter will take his place.

In his sacerdotal prayer, Christ, addressing his Father, says: 'While I was with them, I kept them in thy name' (John 17). Already at the Supper he has told the Apostles that he intends to hand over this task of keeping the whole apostolic college in the truth to one man, Peter: 'Amen I say to *you*: Satan hath desired to sift you as wheat. But I have prayed for *thee*, Peter, that thy faith fail not; and thou being once converted confirm thy brethren' (Luke 22).

From these and several other passages in the Gospels and from the behaviour of Peter as it is recorded in the Acts of the Apostles, it is very plain that there is abundant scriptural justification for applying the term 'Head of the Church', which St. Paul reserves for Christ, to St. Peter and his successors in the primacy.

As one might have inferred from Küng's proposal to scrap the traditional terminology for the Papal primacy, he fails to give due weight to the role of the Roman See in maintaining the unity of the Church. If the Church is not rent asunder by schism and heresy, this is because her Founder built her on the Rock.

Unity in faith is indeed due primarily to the action of the Holy Spirit, but the Holy Spirit achieves this end by the instrumentality of a juridical institution – the Roman primacy.

Küng is therefore astray when he writes: 'The unity of the Catholic Church does not consist only (as was at one time apt to be thought) in the lines joining everything to the one centre, but at the same time, and just as strongly, in the unity of the bishops and the local Churches with one another' [1]. The primary reason why the Church does not disintegrate is that it is built on the Rock. Hence the paramount source of unity in the Church on the juridical level is the communion of each local Church with the Roman See. Their communion with each other plays only a subordinate role, i.e. it does not contribute 'just as strongly' to the unity of the Church.

Similarly, Küng seems to have paid too little attention to the definition of the Council of Florence that the Roman Pontiff is the supreme Teacher of all Christians. He writes: 'The *ecclesia catholica* would not be given credible representation... if some particular individual Church were to impose its special tradition (in devotion, doctrine, law) on the others' [2]. The Roman Church may well allow – indeed she encourages – in other Churches a wide variety of liturgical forms, devotional practices and legal codes, but doctrine is a different matter. The preservation of the deposit of faith has been entrusted in a particular way to her – her Bishop is the only one who enjoys the prerogative of personal infallibility.

Küng's own account of Papal infallibility is unsatisfactory. He writes: 'But the First Vatican Council laid down precisely the *limits* and *conditions* of papal

1. CA. pp. 74–75.
2. CA. p. 56.

"freedom from error" (which would be a better, more accurate way of saying it) and narrowed it down in practice to a few extraordinary cases. It can also be shown from the Acts of the Council how the Pope, when making binding statements of doctrine, must not act separately from the Church but only as representing the whole Church, with whom he must remain in contact' [1].

There are two mis-statements here. First, when the Church defined that the Pope in certain circumstances is infallible, she did not mean merely that he *does not err,* but that he *cannot err.* Secondly, although the Pope in defining does not act separately from the Church – since he defines a doctrine as that which the Church believes – he does not define as 'representing the whole Church', as Küng says. The Papal power of defining infallibly is not delegated but personal. As the First Vatican Council defined, when the Roman Pontiff speaks *ex cathedra,* he defines in virtue of his supreme Apostolic authority, exercising his office as Sheperd and Teacher of all Christians, and his definitions are irreformable of themselves and not because of their acceptance by the Church.

Finally, Küng does less than justice to the ordinary non-infallible teaching authority of the Holy See. He writes: 'The infallibility of the Pope is limited to those few exceptional cases in which the Pope as supreme teacher and sheperd of the Church makes a definitive, binding statement of the Faith for the whole Church... In everything else that he says and does, according to the common teaching of the Church, the Pope can be radically mistaken, though of course he does not have to be mistaken' [2].

This, to say the least, is a curious way of putting

1. CA. p. 201.
2. WB. p. 29.

it: apart from his infallible definitions, the Pope in everything he says can be mistaken, though he does not have to be. In his encyclical *Humani Generis* Pope Pius XII claims for the Holy See a good deal more than this. He writes: 'It is not to be supposed that a position advanced in an encyclical does not, *ipso facto,* claim assent. In writing them, it is true, the Popes do not exercise their teaching authority to the full. But such statements come under the day-to-day teaching of the Church, which is covered by the promise, "He who listens to you, listens to Me" (Luke 10, 16). For the most part, the positions advanced, the duties inculcated, by these encyclical letters are already bound up, under some other title, with the general body of Catholic teaching. And when the Roman Pontiffs go out of their way to pronounce on some subject which has hitherto been controverted, it must be clear to everybody that, in the mind and intention of the Pontiffs concerned, this subject can no longer be regarded as a matter of free debate among theologians' [1].

It is common knowledge that this encyclical has not received a very warm welcome in certain Catholic circles. But it will be authoritative enough for any theologian who has a fully Catholic understanding of the part Christ intended St. Peter and his successors to play in the government of His Kingdom.

2. THE TEACHING AUTHORITY OF THE CHURCH

The Church and Holy Scripture

For classical Protestantism the only definitive norm of faith and morals is the inspired Word of God recorded in the pages of Holy Writ. This written Word is self-

1. *False Trends in Modern Teaching,* ECTS edn. n. 20.

authenticating – as it is preached or read, the soul is moved by the Holy Spirit to receive it in faith, and by this faith, in the merits of Christ, it is justified. To this written Word, tradition and living human teachers are essentially subordinate, and indeed may be dispensed with. The Holy Spirit may make use of such means to bring the Christian to faith and fuller faith in the Word, but He has no need of them.

The Catholic account of the matter is quite different. The Church teaches that Christ ordained that men are to be brought to faith in Him by the preaching of authorized teachers – the Apostles and their successors. He addresses His Word to the believer through the living voice of the Church – the teaching authority of the Pope and the bishops who are in communion with him. Much of what the Church teaches was committed to writing in Apostolic times under the inspiration of the Holy Spirit, and this constitutes the New Testament. In succeeding ages the teaching of the Church is found in the authoritative pronouncements of ecumenical councils and the writings of the Fathers. But these two sources – Scripture and Tradition – while they serve as a guide to the living Church, are not her masters. As Weigel well says, the bishops exercise control in communicating revelation 'by comparing all doctrine with the two instruments of the episcopate, Scripture and Tradition. These things are not over the Church, but are tools in the hands of the bishops . . .' [1].

Küng takes a different view of the matter, and in several passages he describes the subordination of the Church to the Word of God in language more Protestant than Catholic. Take, for example, this suggestion to the Council: 'Few things could be so beneficial to the inner renewal of the Church (and so, indirectly,

1. *Where Do We Differ,* p. 88.

to the cause of reunion) as a manifestation on the part of the Council, of the redemptive significance of the Word of God. It was not for nothing that, even at the Vatican Council, the Holy Scriptures, lying upon a throne in full view of all the bishops, formed, together with the altar, the focal point of the Church there assembled. A solemn confession of faith by the Council in the Word of God, a confession that would leave aside controversies over the exact relation of Scripture to tradition while continuing the positive line of development running through Trent and the Vatican, proclaiming the pre-eminent significance of the Word of God over every word of man, proclaiming its power to pardon, to save, to illuminate, to strengthen, to console – such a declaration could have an extraordinarily beneficial effect on every area of the Church's life . . .' [1].

What good would ensue, we ask, from a confession of faith that was so hopelessly equivocal and expressed in terminology so distinctively Lutheran? 'The redemptive significance of the Word of God' – but where are we to hear this Word? In Holy Scripture, or in the oral authoritative teaching of the Roman Catholic Church? That is the decisive issue on which Luther and the Catholic Church parted company long ago. A confession of faith which left that question in abeyance would resemble all too closely the non-committal communiques which statesmen issue after a conference.

In another passage Küng sets up the Gospel as an independent arbiter, able to settle the Protestant-Catholic controversy. He writes: 'The real question is, *how* is this reunion to be achieved? Only on condition that the *Catholic Church herself* is renewed in conformity with the legitimate demands of the other communions – the legitimate demands of the Orthodox, the

1. CRR. pp. 181–182.

Evangelical, the Anglican, and the Free Church Christians, in the light of the Gospel of Christ. It is the Gospel which must act as judge in our disputes over what is and what is not legitimate in each claim that is made' [1].

To say that it is the Gospel that must act as judge in our disputes with the Orthodox and the Protestants is either empty rhetoric or Lutheranism – or perhaps a claim to authority by the expert in Scriptural exegesis. For it is obvious that the Gospel cannot by itself act as judge, unless one holds, with Luther, that its meaning is self-evident. The Catholic position is that the Gospel must be interpreted. And if one asks: By whom?, the answer is: The Church. Hence it is not the Gospel, but the Church herself, the divinely authorized expounder of the Gospel message, that must act as judge in these disputes between herself and the Protestants.

To reduce the difficulties that block the way to reunion Küng attempts what he describes as 'demolition work', in the hope of removing misunderstandings. Reading these pages [2], one is reminded of wartime stories about sappers who blew up the wrong bridge or airmen who bombed towns in Switzerland.

First he disposes of Catholic misunderstandings about the Protestant view of Councils. Catholics have held that Protestants paid no heed to Councils. This, he assures us, is a mistake, for 'the Reformers did not aim to undermine the authority of councils; indeed they held the authority of the councils of the early Church in high esteem. What they wanted was rather to establish a good foundation for the authority of councils as authority under the word of God' [3].

1. CA p. 108. Cf. *Ibid*. p. 24 for a similar remark.
2. CA. pp. 197 ff.
3. CA. p. 197.

Surely this is rubbish. What sort of authority can a council be said to possess for an individual, when he rejects any of its decisions that do not fit in with his private interpretation of Scripture? Any esteem the Reformers may have had for the councils of the early Church implied no recognition of their authority. They could afford to be patronising to these assemblies of the distant past which had had the good sense to confine their attention to doctrines which the Reformers found no difficulty in accepting, e.g. the Incarnation, the Trinity. Where these councils taught doctrines with which they disagreed, they rejected their teaching without compunction.

Küng's 'demolition' of Protestant misunderstanding of the Catholic position is equally nugatory. Rejecting the notion that 'the Church autocratically appropriates to herself and seizes possession of God's 'revelation', he describes her teaching authority as 'a fulfilment of obedience towards the word of God to which she is subordinated', and concludes, 'God and his word are above, the Church and her word are below'[1].

By 'the word of God' Küng seems to mean here Holy Scripture, for he says that 'the man who bears office has constantly to hear, to receive, to learn the word of God in the human word of Scriptures'[2]. If this is what he means – his treatment of the subject is so confused that it is not easy to discover his meaning – then he is subordinating the living authority of the Church to the written word of Scripture, and presenting this as the Catholic concept of ecclesiastical authority.

Surely the Catholic account of he matter is that since Christ speaks through his Church ('He who hears you, hears Me'), the word of the Church *is* the word

1. CA. p. 198.
2. CA. p. 199.

of God to the world, a word transmitted orally from one generation of the faithful to the next. To speak, as Küng does, of the Church 'desiring in all simplicity to hear and proclaim and expound, not her own word, but the word of God' [1] is to rend asunder what God has joined together.

Dogmatic Definitions of the Faith

Christ our Lord entrusted his revelation to the Church as a sacred deposit to be preserved intact and handed on from generation to generation, and he promised her the assistance of the Holy Spirit in the fulfilment of this task. During the course of ages she has found it necessary from time to time to formulate certain of her doctrines with greater precision in order to exclude heretical interpretations. These precise authoritative formulations of various articles of the faith are *dogmas*. One of the most famous is the dogma defined by the Council of Nicaea (A.D. 325) that Jesus Christ, the Son of God, is *consubstantial* with the Father.

The essential function of these dogmatic definitions is to serve as precise expressions of divine truth; they are statements, as adequate as the Church can make them, of the content of one or other of the divine mysteries. Although they regulate usage, they are primarily affirmations about what is. The terms employed are necessarily used in an analogous sense, but the human mind can grasp their positive content clearly enough to see what is to be believed and how it differs from the heresy. Thus it conveys something to the human mind to say that the Son is of one substance with the Father, a relationship evidently different from that

1. CA. p. 198.

of subordination which the Arians affirmed.

Are dogmatic definitions subject to revision? It depends on what one means by revision. There can be no revision in the sense of abandoning positions previously adopted. This was defined by the First Vatican Council: 'If anyone shall say that it is possible that, as knowledge advances, dogmas proposed by the Church should be given a different meaning from that which the Church has understood and understands, let him be anathema' [1].

If revision be taken to mean progress to a formulation that is more precise, this is not only possible, it has frequently occurred. This, as Küng points out is the teaching of the encyclical *Humani Generis*. He writes: 'Being words with human limitations – though, thanks to the assistance of the Holy Spirit, promised to the Church, always teaching truth and not error – the words of a council can, even according to *Humani Generis*, be clarified, supplemented, and brought to greater perfection. St. Augustine goes so far as to use the word *emendare*, "to correct" in this connection' [2].

However, a number of modern theologians, Küng being one, interpret 'revision' in a more radical sense. They regard dogmas as essentially human and historical formulations of Divine truth, statements made to the men of one particular age in concepts appropriate to that age, but requiring to be radically altered to make them intelligible to the men of a subsequent age. Thus Küng writes: 'The doctrine of the Church, as to its concrete form, is immersed in history and to this extent subject to culpable and inculpable deformations, and must therefore to this extent be constantly renewed and reformed' [3]. Similarly, he cites as a point on which

1. Denzinger, op. cit. n. 1818.
2. CA. p. 60.
3. Cf. CRR. pp. 53–54.

Catholic and Protestant theology have manifestly come closer to each other, 'the concept of dogma as essentially historical and conditioned by time, and hence susceptible of improvement' [1].

It is simply not true to say that Catholic dogma is 'immersed in history' and 'essentially historical'. The Church in formulating her dogmas enjoys the direct and special guidance of the Holy Spirit and hence the formulas she finds are not wholly conditioned by the intellectual atmosphere of the time. They are meta-historical.

In the encyclical *Humani Generis* Pope Pius XII condemned this historicism. He wrote: 'Some are for whittling away the meaning of doctrines to the utmost limit. Dogma must be disentangled from the forms of expression which have so long been accepted in the schools, from the philosophical notions which find favour with Catholic teachers; there must be a return, in our exposition of Catholic doctrine, to the language of Scripture and of the Fathers. Privately they cherish the hope that dogma, when thus stripped of the elements which they regard as external to divine revelation, may be usefully compared with the theological opinions of other bodies, separated from the unity of the Church; this might lead, by degrees, to a levelling-up between Catholic doctrines and the views of those who disagree with us...

'There is no absurdity, then, they say, rather there is a strict necessity about the idea that theology should constantly be exchanging old concepts for new, as times keep on altering and it finds, in the gradual development of philosophy, new tools ready to its hand. The same divine truth, they tell us, may be expressed on the human side in two different ways, nay, in two ways which in a sense contradict one

1. CA. p. 26.

48

another, and yet really mean the same thing. And they go on to say that the history of dogma consists in that and nothing else; in giving some account of the various successive forms under which revealed truth has appeared, corresponding to the various theories and speculations which the centuries have brought with them' [1].

It is fairly plain that Küng's theology of dogma is tainted with the relativism indicated in *Humani Generis,* for he says that dogmatic definitions, being essentially historical, stand in need of correction. He writes: 'As human and historical formulations it is of the very nature of the definitions of the Church to be open to correction and to stand in need of correction. Progress in dogma is not always necessarily an organic development' [2].

Earlier he has used the word 'correction' to mean 'greater precision or clarification' (in the sense of St. Augustine's *emendare*) but the word seems to mean more than that here. For if 'progress in dogma is not always an organic development', it follows that the Church in defining doctrine may depart from the fullness of truth, using formulas that are out of harmony with revelation.

In another passage he distinguishes between the divine element in dogma, which is irreformable, and the human element which is reformable. He writes: 'In doctrine as elsewhere we have to distinguish between what is given, *irreformably,* by God through Jesus Christ in the Holy Spirit, and what comes, *reformably,* from men. And what was said before applies equally to doctrine: the reformable and the irreformable cannot be adequately represented as on two separate levels. *Every* dogma of the Church

---

1. *False Trends in Modern Teaching,* ECTS., nn. 14–15.
2. CA. p. 205.

expresses at the same time both the irreformable divine revelation and what is human and reformable. There are indeed, in the Church's dogma, certain abiding constants which remain in every possible formula, through every variation of thought or image or manner of speech, which are given us by God's revelation itself (as for example the godhead and manhood of Jesus Christ), but there are not, properly speaking, any irreformable *areas* in what is of human, ecclesiastical formulation' [1].

It is not easy to determine exactly what Küng means by this. But he seems to be saying that the only irreformable elements in the Church's doctrine are the great elementary truths that are explicitly contained in New Testament, such as the divinity of Jesus Christ; any elements that are of ecclesiastical origin are human and reformable. He seems unwilling to allow that God speaks throught the Church and guarantees the correctness of her dogmatic definitions.

To illustrate his contention that the Church's dogmatic definitions are inadequate, Küng cites the treatment by the Council of Trent of Luther's theory of justification. Trent, he maintains, failed to do justice to the kernel of truth contained in Luther's error. He writes: 'Ecclesiastical definition struck at error, but did not explicitly except from its condemnation the core of truth in the error; this means that the true condemnation of error seemed to the other side a false condemnation of truth. A definition of the Church, for example, condemned *sola fides* in so far as it was an empty, presumptuous, self-righteous belief in justification; it did not define with sufficient clarity what can also be truly meant by *sola fides;* faith in the good and true sense which puts all its trust in God alone' [2].

1. CRR. pp. 115–116.
2. CA. p. 207.

Whether the Lutheran *sola fides* can rightly be called self-righteous is doubtful, but that does not concern us here. What does concern us is Küng's assertion that Trent did not explicitly except from condemnation what was true in Luther's teaching. It suffices to read canons 1, 2, 3, 10 and 33 of the Session on justification, to see that that Council explicitly affirmed such truths as were to be found in Luther's creed – man's absolute dependence on the grace of Christ for justification, good works, perseverance, and the meriting of eternal life. What Trent provided was a *balanced* account of justification, which did full justice to the various aspects of this mystery – the kind of dogmatic definition which Küng tells us he would like to see in other contexts. Indeed, in another work he admits as much, for he writes: 'The decree on justification, which is the glory of the Council, accepts what is valid in the Reformers' position to a surprising degree' [1].

We find evidence of Küng's cavalier attitude towards the dogmatic definitions of earlier Councils in a passage in which he calmly assumes that the main points of doctrine on which Catholics and Protestants disagree have not been settled by Trent and First Vatican. He writes: 'It would also not be opportune to settle differences of doctrine between the individual Christian denominations – these will have to be gone over slowly and thoroughly by the theologians from the exegetical, historical and dogmatic points of view. The Council cannot replace the work of the theologians, and in any case, a premature attempt to resolve highly controversial issues of doctrine would do the gravest disservice to the ecumenical cause' [2].

An attempt to resolve highly controversial issues of doctrine that have been resolved four hundred years

1. CRR. p. 78.
2. CA. pp. 109–110.

ago would not be premature, but anachronistic. The theologian undertaking such a task would be a kind of Rip Van Winkle, who fell asleep in 1534 and has just woken up in 1964.

If there were any doubt that what Küng has in mind in the passage just quoted is the differences in doctrine that caused the split at the Reformation, this is removed by the following passage from a later work: 'Nor can it be the task of the Council to decide the controversial questions that broke out between the different Christian confessions at the Reformation. We are not yet ready to carry out such an operation with sufficient depth and balance' [1].

This passage contains a *suggestio falsi,* viz. that Lutheranism and Calvinism were going concerns at the time of the Reformation instead of heresies which came into being at that time; and a *suppressio veri,* because the controversial questions which broke out at that time (the nature of justification, the nature and number of the sacraments, the Real Presence, the sacrificial character of the Mass, the nature of faith and its relation to reason, the primacy and infallibility of the Roman Pontiff) have all been definitively settled by Trent and First Vatican.

Tactics of this sort, however they may appear to favour ecumenism, do the gravest disservice to the ecumenical cause, for they must lead to disillusionment when our separated brethren discover that gates which they have been led to believe are open have long since been closed. As Greenstock says: 'So far as Catholics are concerned, the Decrees of Trent set the seal of infallibility on the orthodox Catholic doctrine of the time and nothing can change that. It is one of the points which we must be prepared to discuss with our separated brethren in the ecumeni-

1. CA. p. 215.

cal movement, and we must be prepared to do so without selling the past' [1].

Two Ways of Squaring the Circle in Dogma

The reconciliation of incompatible notions like 'square' and 'circle' has never been a particularly fruitful undertaking, but some thinkers, in the interests of what they conceive to be ecumenism, have been trying their hand at it. The task may be undertaken in either of two ways. The first way is to maintain that 'square' and 'circle' are two different names for geometrical figures that are essentially identical. From this it follows that which term we employ is simply a matter of usage; at one time custom or authority will decree that the figure has four sides, at another that it is circular.

The second way of resolving the contradiction is to create a composite term 'squircle' which will serve to designate both geometrical figures indifferently.

The terms employed in dogmatic theology are different from geometrical terms, but the illustration drawn from geometry will serve to throw light on the parallel dialectical processes in dogmatic theology.

Küng provides a sample of the first method in the following passage: 'Faith can be the same though formulas are not only different but (as is shown by the history of the dogma of the Trinity) mutually opposed. Behind the different and *contradictory* formulations of faith stand different physiological, psychological, aesthetic, linguistic, logical, ethnological, historical, ideological, philosophical and religious presuppositions...

'Is it any wonder that Christians holding *one* faith should often have failed to understand each other, and

1. Art. cit. p. 612.

cast each other out when they could have been at one with each other? It often happened that all that was noticed in other people's statements was what was missing, while all that was noticed in one's own was what was there; that the *content* of truth in one's own formula and the lack of it in the other were all that one took notice of...

'The Church cannot, indeed, be indifferent to formulas of faith, since faith itself expresses itself through them. She will indeed rightly insist that it is not for everyone at all times to formulate everything, or the Church will be invaded by misunderstandings, disorder, quarrels, divisions and downright chaos. Hence she will, indeed, in the service of the one Faith, have at certain times to regulate usage by forbidding certain formulas and proposing others. Convinced that because of the Lord's sustaining word and intercession, the Church of the earlier centuries, too, stood in the same Faith, she will indeed respect the formulas of that earlier Church as utterances of the one unchanging Faith, and not reject or condemn them even when they are formulated in a way that seems to be different, inverted or even inapposite. The Church will indeed thus discern and hold fast to the one unchanging Faith under all the various formulas of the various centuries. But nevertheless and at the same time she will, in this age of ecumenical encounter with other Christian communions, strive to discover that one same Faith under the different and opposed formulas that the others use so as to accord to them, with the greatest possible openness and readiness to understand, difference in *formula*, so long as they have the same *faith*' [1].

This is a long quotation but the passage is an

---

1. CA. pp. 204–205. *Contradictory* (italics mine). Cf. *Humani Generis* n. 15 quoted *Supra* p. 48–9.

important one for the light it throws on Küng's attitude to dogmatic formulas. The thought and expression are a little obscure. This, so far as I can make him out, is what Küng means: 'By his presence in the Church, Christ ensures that she abides always in the one unchanging Faith, but when it comes to finding formulas to express the faith, He provides her with no help at all. Left to her own devices, and influenced by the psychological and other presuppositions of her members, she will employ in her solemn definitions terms that are inverted and inapposite, so that what she called a square in the sixteenth century, she will in the twentieth define to be a circle. This is quite in order, because her definitions merely regulate usage; and the statement that such-and-such is a square simply means that all her children must for the time being use this term when speaking of it. She will be compelled to disavow those who persist in speaking of it as a circle, even though, later on, moved by exegetical, historical and dogmatic considerations she may herself define it to be a circle.

'When therefore Luther expressed his doctrine in one formula and the Council of Trent in defining Catholic faith employed a contradictory formula, they could well have been using different terms to express the same faith. And in this age of ecumenical encounter we may discover that there is no compelling reason why we should not alter our usage and employ Lutheran terminology to express the one unchanging Faith. Had this been done in the sixteenth century, it might not have been necessary to cast our Lutheran brethren out of the Church'.

In this clarification I have dotted some of Küng's i's and crossed his t's, making explicit what he has left implicit, but otherwise it seems a fair rendering of his thought.

The second method of squaring the dogmatic circle is to devise an ambiguous formula (corresponding to 'squircle'), to which Protestants and Catholics could both subscribe. This is the method Küng suggests in a passage where he warns the theologian of 'the grave dangers which may deprive his theological work of its ecumenical fruit' [1]. The third of these dangers is 'the danger of making excessive demands for theological agreement. It follows from the last point that in working to come together in theology we must not demand an exaggerated degree of agreement. Otherwise we should, in our ecumenical discussions, be requiring some totally impossible kind of agreement which would make reunion itself impossible' [2]. Küng then proceeds to quote some remarks of Karl Rahner that are, he says, 'extremely important with reference to ecumenical discussion'. Since Rahner is refuting those who would demand an excessive measure of agreement, on the ground of 'the essential impossibility of reaching absolute certainty about our ultimate interior identity of conviction', we may fairly assume that in quoting Rahner here, Küng has made Rahner's thought his own.

Rahner concludes his remarks with a word of praise for equivocal dogmatic formulas. He writes: 'Perhaps those formulae of union in ancient times which seem somewhat artificial and political in their construction were not by any means the worst. What seems like a purely verbal and artificial unity may often be the one and only thing possible in face of the inconceivable Mystery: to find a formula which leaves to each side its own irreducible contribution to the controversy and to its solution, while requiring both to see and express what was well recognized by the other but overlooked

1. CRR. p. 117.
2. CRR. p. 119.

or not clearly seen by himself, so that the other shall see that he holds it too. We should not then say at once of every formula of agreement: Oh, yes, but go a little deeper into it and discrepancies will soon appear; the general terms in which it is stated are simply hiding them! As though we could not have the very same suspicion about all the unity within the Catholic Church!' [1].

As an example of a formula of union that was artificial and political in its construction we may take that which was adopted by the Council of Rimini-Seleucia in 359 under pressure from the Emperor Constantius. At Nicaea the Church had defined as an article of Catholic faith the doctrine that the Son is consubstantial *(homousios)* with the Father. The Arians, who denied the divinity of the Son, steadfastly refused to accept this term, urging, among other things, that it is not to be found in Holy Scripture. They were, however, prepared to admit that the Son is like *(homoios)* the Father. Obviously this term could bear a Catholic interpretation, for if the Son is consubstantial with the Father, He must be like Him. The Emperor decided that in the interests of Christian unity both parties should accept this ambiguous term as an adequate expression of the Christian faith. The western bishops met at Rimini in May, the eastern in Seleucia in October, and although the orthodox bishops had some misgivings, both parts of the Council bowed to the wishes of the Emperor and employed the term *homoios* in the official conciliar statement of the faith. This is the Council which, years afterwards, provoked St. Jerome's comment: 'The whole world groaned to find itself Arian'. The saint was using hyperbole, but plainly he did not think highly of vague formulas used to reconcile the irreconcilable.

1. CRR. p. 121.

Nor have these vague formulas found much favour with Catholic theologians since St. Jerome's day. Indeed, it would be hard to find any theologians, whether Catholic or Protestant, apart from these exponents of a spurious ecumenism, who would be prepared to admit that 'what seems like a purely verbal and artificial unity may often be the one and only thing possible in the face of the inconceivable Mystery'. By definition a theologian is one who is committed to the task of expressing in human concepts the inconceivable Mystery. Theology is a discourse about God. In a discourse one uses words as symbols to express concepts; in theological discourse the theologian has to choose those concepts which will serve to express divine realities. Silence before the inconceivable Mystery may be all very well for the mystic. It will not do for the theologian, who has to expound the faith in terms that are intelligible and as precise as he can make them.

It may help us to see more clearly the weakness in Rahner's position if we consider a formula of union, artificial and political in construction, that was drawn up in more recent times. This is the Thirty-nine Articles, drawn up in language so ambiguous as to be acceptable to all but a small minority of Englishmen and serving as the doctrinal basis of a national church that would be as comprehensive as possible. As a consequence of this policy there is a wide range of belief within the confines of the Anglican Church.

Rahner maintains that any doubts one might entertain about the unity of faith resulting from such compromise formulas as the *homoios* of Seleucia-Rimini (and we add, the Thirty-nine Articles) could be equally well-founded in the case of the Catholic Church. The vital fact which Rahner has overlooked is that the Holy Spirit is present in the Church, assist-

ing the Pope and bishops in their work of teaching
and the faithful in their assent to this teaching and so
keeping the Church in the unity of faith. He was not
with the bishops at Seleucia-Rimini nor is He with
the Anglican Church as such.

Is the Church too negative in the exercise of her teaching office?

Küng is very critical of the attitude of earlier Councils
of the Church, Trent in particular. He writes: 'One
may wonder whether ecumenical councils might not
have done better to concern themselves with a positive
proclamation of the Gospel than with negative con-
demnations (remembering e.g. the Fourth Lateran
Council and the positive demands of the Waldenses) [1].

Elsewhere [2] Küng himself admits that the condemnation of error is sometimes necessary. What he does
not seem to have grasped is that the condemnation
of an error implies the affirmation of the opposite truth.
This indeed supposes the logical principle that contradictory statements are mutually exclusive, so that if
one is false the other is necessarily true; but as we
have seen [3], this is a principle which Küng may not
be willing to accept.

The Council of Trent, Küng maintains, was much too
negative in its attitude towards the Protestants. He
writes: 'When at last the Council of Trent did meet,
Luther was already dead and no Protestants made
their appearance at it. The frontiers had hardened
and the Council gave sanction to that hardening. No
one denies that the Council of Trent did a colossal

1. CA. p. 210.
2. CA. p. 12, 213.
3. Cf. Supra p. 53–4.

work of reform within the Church and set the Catholic Church firmly on the upward path after the decadence of the Renaissance. But it brought no reunion of separated Christians. The immediate aim of the Council was defence, condemnation and expulsion' [1].

The aim of Trent in the doctrinal field was to define clearly certain articles of Catholic faith which Luther, Calvin and others had denied, so that henceforward there could be no doubt about the Church's teaching on these points. As Küng wrote in an earlier work: 'In the sphere of doctrine the purpose of Trent was to define Catholic teaching against that of the Reformers' [2]. The frontier between Lutheranism and the faith was sharply drawn quite early and Luther publicly acknowledged that he had crossed it when he burnt the bull 'Exsurge' in December 1520.

The immediate aim of the Council was not and could not have been reunion. Its task was to re-affirm as clearly as possible the ancient faith, the only basis on which reunion is conceivable. To describe its immediate aim as expulsion is nonsense, since the heretics whose views it condemned had long since left the Church and were bent on destroying her. Küng's account of Trent and the Reformation reminds one of those histories of the Russian Revolution in which the West gets all the blame because it treated the Communist leaders with suspicion.

Does the Church need a New Theology?

Christ revealed the mysteries of the Kingdom of God in an unsystematic way, speaking, as occasion offered, now of one aspect of this heavenly realm, now of

1. CA. p. 33.
2. CRR. p. 78.

another, using parables to describe its origin, growth, and consummation, and gradually revealing His own place in it. To those who received Him in faith He promised a new form of life, the life of sanctifying grace. Living by this life, man is introduced into a whole new living world, the world of the supernatural, a new order of reality for him to contemplate.

When the human mind is confronted with reality, it seeks to understand it, to discover the order which it knows must be embodied in what at first sight seems chaotic and disorderly. So it proceeds by a slow, laborious process from the naive intuition of reality to science. The order that emerges from a comprehensive survey and close scrutiny of the inanimate world is what gives their scientific character to such sciences as physics, chemistry, astronomy, and geology. To discern the order that exists in the world of living forms, plant and animal, is the task of the sciences of botany and zoology.

To discover and set out in systematic form the order that exists in the supernatural world is the function of the science of theology. The subject-matter which the theologian investigates is the deposit of faith which Christ has entrusted to his Church. His task is to penetrate more deeply into the mysteries, in order to see more clearly the content of each and its connection with all the others. Possessing the faith and submissive to the authority of the Church, the theologian endeavours to reach a profounder understanding of the intellectual riches in which he shares through faith. In St. Anselm's lapidary phrase, theology is 'fides quaerens intellectum' – faith in quest of understanding.

In his quest for understanding the theologian uses such intellectual tools as will serve his purpose. Since the Christian revelation was made in a particular historical context – as the culmination of a long process of divine revelation that centred finally on Israel – to understand this revelation properly the theologian must have some knowledge of its context. For this he needs some knowledge of philology, history and comparative religion.

To come to an understanding of the content of the revelation itself he must employ philosophy, since the revelation is concerned with God and man and the relations between them, and the concepts which we employ when we are thinking of such matters as these are philosophical. True, the average man uses such concepts without adverting to their philosophical character – as M. Jourdain spoke prose without being aware of it – but the philosopher, who has the last word in such matters, recognizes them as implicitly philosophical.

For example, it is Catholic doctrine that in the unity of the Godhead there is a Trinity of persons, and in Christ, only one person, but two natures and two operations of will. If the theologian is to give an intelligible account of these doctrines, he must explain what is meant by 'nature', 'person', and 'operation of will'; and for this he must make use of notions derived from philosophy.

Hence it is plain that the soundness of a theologian's theory will depend in no small measure on the soundness of the philosophy he employs in its construction. Of some systems of philosophy the theologian can make no use at all. Such, for example would be the system of Dialectical Materialism. To use this in the construction of a system of theology would be like using a horse and cart for a trip to the moon. Other systems of philosophy that are likewise unusable in theology, because of their incompatibility with Christian revelation, are Cartesian Subjectivism, Humean

Scepticism (either in its native form or revamped as Logical Positivism), or Kantian Idealism.

Christian theology, of which we can trace the beginnings in the Epistle to the Romans and the Apostles' Creed, has developed through the ages under the watchful eye of the Church, for though the construction of theological systems is not her essential task – that is the preaching of the Gospel – she cannot be indifferent to theology. Pope and bishops make use of theology in defending and expounding the faith, and the Church has sometimes made use of terms derived from theology in defining the articles of faith. Moreover, systematic theology enables the Church to discharge her debt to the wise by presenting the faith as a well-ordered and comprehensive view of reality, well able to compete in the intellectual market with any system of philosophy.

Of the various systems that Christian thinkers have elaborated in the course of history, the Church has expressed a decided preference for that of St. Thomas Aquinas. In every century since the thirteenth the Popes have praised his teaching in the highest terms, and in the last hundred years they have committed the Church more and more to his doctrine. One of the first things Pope Leo XIII did on his elevation to the Papacy was to issue the encyclical *Aeterni Patris* calling on all Christian thinkers to take St. Thomas as their master. 'The Church', said Pope Benedict XV, 'has made the doctrine of Thomas her own'. According to the Code of Canon Law, all those who are preparing for the priesthood must study philosophy and theology according to the method, system and basic principles of St. Thomas. Nor has there in recent years been any change in the attitude of the Papacy. Praising St. Thomas's philosophy (and by implication his theology) Pope Pius XII wrote in the encyclical

Humani Generis: 'One thing is clearly established by the long experience of the ages – that St. Thomas's philosophical system is an unrivalled method, either for putting the beginner through his paces, or for the investigation of the most recondite truths; moreover, that his teaching seems to chime in, by a kind of pre-established harmony, with divine revelation – no surer way to safeguard the first principles of the faith, and turn the results of later, healthy developments to good advantage' [1]. Finally we may quote Pope John XXIII, who said in 1960: 'If all these things that we desire so ardently are to come about, the first thing necessary is to study the works of St. Thomas carefully. And so we are very interested in seeing a steady growth in the number of people who find enlightenment and learning in the works of the Angelic Doctor' [2].

It requires no great perspicacity to see that Küng does not share the sentiments of the Sovereign Pontiffs towards St. Thomas. Thus, he includes Thomism in his 'sorrowful litany' of things wrong with the Church, such as scandals among the clergy and the pilgrimage racket [3].

He is nowhere explicit on the point, but if I read him aright he objects to the theology of St. Thomas on the grounds that it is out-of-date, insufficiently biblical and a hindrance to reunion. What he wants is a theology that is exclusively biblical and owes nothing to Aristotelian philosophy, a theology that is philosophically so uncommitted that it could equally well incorporate Vedanta philosophy of Bantu Idealism [4] – a theology, in short, that it is no longer

1. *False Trends in Modern Teaching* ECTS, nr. 31.
2. *The Pope Speaks* 6, (1960), p. 327.
3. CRR. p. 158.
4. Cf. CA. p. 250.

a theology. For before the theologian embarks on the work of creating a theology, he must choose some system of philosophy. Mere eclecticism will get him nowhere. This means that if he chooses to use materials from Vedanta Philosophy or Bantu Idealism, he will have to subject them to philosophical criticism. And then the question is: What philosophical principles is he going to employ in this work of criticism? In his principles are those of St. Thomas, he can be fairly confident that his theology will be in harmony with the Catholic faith, since the Church has signified her approval of these. If he uses any others, he is very liable to go astray. As Pope St. Pius X said, he who departs from the teaching of St. Thomas in metaphysics, even by one step, will hardly avoid falling into grievous error.

In his criticism of systematic theology, Küng creates for his target a man of straw. He writes: 'Now, it is beyond question that theologians have acted, all too often, as though it were their job, and within their power, to find some definite explanatory, abstract formula for every single item in revelation, when they should often have been humbly content to let it rest in the variety of scriptural utterance' [1].

Some theologians have acted in the manner Küng describes, but he generalizes – 'theologians' – and, as a general statement, what he says is false. The great theologians cherish no such ambition as he attributes to them. On the other hand, they have not been content to let the doctrines of the faith rest in the variety of biblical utterance, for this would be to abandon their theological task, which is, precisely, to coordinate the various items of revelation. The view that a theologian should be content with the variety of biblical utterance is the error of biblicism.

1. CRR. p. 117.

That Küng's conception of theology is fairly close to biblicism is clear from the following passage in which he repudiates systematic theology in favour of the biblical variety. He writes: 'By theology is meant here not that unscriptural theology which discourses at large, *non*-definitively, on all possible and impossible subjects, and naturally on ecumenical councils as well, but that Christian theology which recognizes itself as bound to the revelation of God in Jesus Christ, and from *that* source is called to make definitive pronouncements' [1]. Once again we have a caricature of systematic theology, which is damned as 'unscriptural'. The question the systematic theologian would put to Küng is: Where is Christian theology to find this revelation of God in Jesus Christ? In Holy Scripture, or in the teaching of the Church?

In view of these pronouncements, one can accept only with great reserve Küng's statement that 'a less scholastic and more scriptural theology is urgently necessary' [2]. The question is: How much less scholastic and how much more scriptural? Is the scholastic or systematic element to be reduced to vanishing point, in accordance with tenets of biblicism? If, as seems likely, this is what Küng means, he would leave the Church without a theology.

On this subject of biblicism, Weigel pertinently comments: 'Much as I rejoice in the progress so brilliantly made by Catholic scholars in the last twenty years, yet as a theologian I have qualms. Of course it is gladly admitted by Catholic theologians that the more you know about the Bible, the more you will know about revelation, and that is what any theologian organizes into an intelligent synthesis. But the Bible students show a tendency which would impoverish theo-

1. CA. pp. 43–44.
2. CA. p. 258.

logy. Unconsciously the scripturists show an impatience with any theology which is not all but exclusively biblical.

'The matter has been put most clearly by a Protestant, Walter von Loewenich, and I doubt if any Catholic would go as far as he does. He thinks that scientific exegesis is the only way to achieve an understanding of Scripture. A theological interpretation, other than the one indicated by scientific philology, is for him spurious, deriving from and leading to mere mythology...

As I have said, it seems impossible for any Catholic to go so far, and yet there are signs that some Catholic exegetes do move along with Loewenich, up to some indefinite point short of his conclusions' [1].

The theology of St. Thomas, as everyone who has studied it closely is well aware, is thoroughly scriptural, and it may be doubted whether our Tübingen theologians have as profound and comprehensive acquaintance with the sacred text as the Angelic Doctor. But even if Küng acknowledged this, he would still feel compelled to repudiate his theology because he regards it as 'static', a mediaeval strait-jacket quite unsuited to these times of ecumenical encounter. If we are to work effectively for reunion, we must scrap scholastic theology and adopt ecumenical theology. 'Theological work for reunion', Küng writes, 'may be crippled... by having insufficient intellectual energy to break out of one's own theological scheme or system, constructed perhaps decades ago and defended ever since, as one must do if one is to remain ever open to the ever greater truth of divine revelation' [2].

We live in the age of the trade-in. One keeps a car for a year or two and then exchanges it for the

1. *Where Do We Differ?* p. 39.
2. CRR. p. 118.

new and improved model. What more natural than that we should do likewise in theology? Why keep a thirteenth-century system of theology when you can exchange it for the up-to-date model that is all the rage: ecumenical theology? As Küng remarks, in the style of Madison Avenue: 'Ecumenical theology is now sought after. Ecumenical theology is now in demand; theologians are being positively urged to replace "static" theology with a theology "on the march"; a theology of mutual encounter, in which truth is illuminated by understanding love, instead of a state-of-siege theology, with love subordinated to so-called truth. A theology, in fact, which is a preparation for reunion' [1].

In the Middle Ages the primary object of theology was to seek a deeper understanding of the truth revealed by God and to express it as fully and precisely as possible, just as motor-cars used to be regarded as primarily a means of transport. But our ecumenical enthusiasts have changed all that. Theology is now to be ecumenical, oriented primarily towards reunion and mutual loving encounter. (Hurry along and buy our 1964 model now so eagerly sought after. With this automobile, the newest creation of our Detroit studios, the young bachelor can enter with confidence in the matrimonial stakes!)

A new theology, on the march. But whither? Elementary prudence warns us against buying a pig in a poke. So the wise theologian, before he accepts the invitation to break out of his theological system, will want to know much more about this ecumenical theology which he is urged to take in exchange. He has read of mad stampedes like the South Sea Bubble and of Phineas Barnum's axiom about one being born every minute, and like the man from Missouri he wants to be shown the article he is being asked to

1. CA. p. 36.

buy. On closer inspection this ecumenical theology turns out to be no theology at all, but simply an attitude of open-mindedness, of receptivity to the ever greater truth of revelation and readiness to recognize value in the insights of our separated brethren. So the 1964 model turns out to be no new car, but only a few accessories. A wise man will keep his car.

More especially because it carries the Church's guarantee. As we read in the encyclical *Humani Generis:* 'It is evident that the Church cannot be tied down to any philosophy which has had a brief moment of popularity. But the framework which has been built up, over a course of centuries, by the common consent of Catholic teachers, cannot be dismissed as resting on a flimsy foundation of that sort. It rests on principles, on ideas, which have been inferred from a just apprehension of created things; and in the making of such inferences the star of truth, divinely revealed, has shone out to the human mind through the Church's agency. No wonder if some of these conceptions have been used, and hallowed in their use, by the General Councils, after such a fashion that they cannot, without impiety, be abandoned.

'So numerous they are, and so important, these theological concepts which have been hammered out and polished with such care, in order to express, with ever-increasing accuracy, the truths in which we believe. It is a process that has often cost centuries of labour, carried out by men of no common intellectual attainment, under the watchful eye of Authority, with light and leading from the Holy Spirit. Must they now fall into disuse, be cast aside, be robbed of all their meaning? Are we to substitute for them guesswork of our own, vague and impermanent fashions of speech, borrowed from our up-to-date philosophies, which today live and will feed the over tomorrow?

That were indeed the height of imprudence; the whole of dogma would thus become no better than a reed shaken by the wind. Treat with disrespect the terms and concepts which have been used by scholastic theologians, and the result, invariably, is to take all the force out of what is called "speculative" theology' [1].

3. THE EUCHARIST

Doctrine

The centre of the life of the Church on earth is the Holy Eucharist, in which Christ, truly present under the appearances of bread and wine, renews the sacrificial offering of Himself which He made on the Cross, and communicates the fruits of His Passion to the Church, which shares in His offering, and in an especial manner to those who receive Him worthily in Communion.

This faith in the Holy Eucharist is one of the features that most sharply distinguishes Catholicism from Protestantism. In the well-known judgement of Augustine Birrell, the Mass is what makes the difference between a Catholic country and a Protestant one: 'It is the Mass that matters'.

There had been sporadic attacks on the Catholic doctrine of the Eucharist during the Middle Ages, but with the Reformation there was a massive onslaught. Luther began the assault, denying transubstantiation and the sacrificial character of the Mass, and soon he was joined by a host of others – Zwingli, Oecolampadius, Calvin and many more – who all agreed with him on these two points, however much they disagreed with him and with one another on the reality and nature of Christ's presence in the Eucharist.

1. *False Trends in Modern Teaching*, ECTS, nn. 16–17.

At Trent the Church condemned these manifold errors and reaffirmed in unequivocal terms her age-old teaching on this sacrament. Here are the canons in which she dealt with the principal points in dispute:

'If anyone shall deny that in the sacrament of the most holy Eucharist there is contained truly, really, and substantially the body and blood of our Lord Jesus Christ, together with His soul and divinity, i.e. the whole Christ; but shall say He is in this sacrament only as in a sign, or an image, or by His power, let him be anathema.

'If anyone shall say that in the holy sacrament of the Eucharist the substance of bread and wine remains together with the body and blood of our Lord Jesus Christ, and shall deny that marvellous and unique conversion of the whole substance of the bread into His body and of the whole substance of the wine into His blood, the species of bread and wine alone remaining, a conversion which the Catholic Church, employing the most suitable terminology, calls transubstantiation, let him be anathema.

'If anyone shall say that in the Mass a true and proper sacrifice is not offered to God, or that the offering consists in nothing else than the giving of Christ as food, let him be anathema.

'If anyone shall say that the sacrifice of the Mass is merely a sacrifice of praise and thanksgiving, or the bare commemoration of the sacrifice completed on the Cross, but is not propitiatory; or that it profits only him who receives the sacrament, and should not be offered for the living and the dead, for sins, the punishment due to sin, satisfaction, or other necessities, let him be anathema' [1].

The teaching of the Council of Trent on the sacrifice

---

1. Denzinger, op. cit. nn. 883, 884, 948, 950.

of the Mass is set out in greater length by Pope Pius XII in the encyclical *Mediator Dei*. There the Pope explains how the Mass is a sacrifice offered by Christ, the High Priest, who 'does what He had already done on the Cross, offering Himself to the eternal Father as a most acceptable victim' [1].

The same Pontiff in his encyclical *Humani Generis* mentions among the poisonous fruits which the spirit of novelty has borne in almost every sphere of theology doubts about the doctrines of transubstantiation and the Real Presence. He writes: 'You will find men arguing that the doctrine of Transubstantiation ought to be revised, depending as it does on a conception of substance which is now out af date. The real presence of Christ in the Holy Eucharist is thus reduced to a kind of symbolic communication, the consecrated species being no more than an effectual sign of Christ's spiritual presence, and of his close union with his faithful members in the Mystical Body' [2].

The views expressed by Küng on the Holy Eucharist are not nearly so extreme as those castigated in *Humani Generis*. Nevertheless one cannot help wondering whether his acceptance of the solemn definitions of Trent is as unreserved as one would expect of a Catholic theologian, for he seems a little unhappy with the doctrine of transubstantiation and the terms in which he customarily describes the Mass include no reference to its sacrificial character.

Thus he lists among Catholic steps towards a fulfilment of the Protestant demands: 'Significant increase in theological attention to the Eucharist as a memorial celebration; as a banquet; as the community worship of the people, who have, in their own fashion, a priesthood; more balanced interpretation of transubstantia-

1. *Christian Worship* ECTS, nn. 70–83.
2. *False Trends in Modern Teaching*, ECTS, n. 26.

tion and sacrifice...' [1].

What does Küng mean by 'a more balanced inter-pretation of transubstantiation and sacrifice?' Surely in the Holy Eucharist either there is transubstantiation or there is not. Is a 'more balanced' interpretation one that explains away the definition of Trent?

Similarly when we read that 'A great deal of fresh thought needs to be given to the theology of the Eucharist, and in particular with reference to its commemorative aspect, to the doctrine of transubstan-tiation, to the sacrificial aspect of the Mass and the problems involved in it' [2], we are entitled to inquire how much attention these fresh thinkers intend to pay to the definitions of Trent.

The indications are that Trent and its definitions are likely to play a minor role in the thought of our ecumenical theologians. Consider, for example, the following passage on Counter-Reformation theology: 'The theology of the Counter-Reformation was in many ways biassed and of a very dubious nature, especially where its teaching on the Mass was con-cerned. For example, the commemorative aspect of the Mass and its character as a banquet, both of which were still in prominence in the Middle Ages, were neglected, whereas its sacrificial aspect was subject to overemphasis. Now it is the concept of the sacrifice and the way in which it should be presented and brought home to the people which pose numerous questions which have still to be resolved. In any renewal of the Canon, the original proportions of the eucharistic prayer and its earliest perspectives would have to be taken carefully into account in the light of Holy Scripture' [3].

1. CRR. pp. 106–107.
2. CA. p. 120.
3. CA. pp. 142–143.

Since the Reformers, as Clark says, 'were at one in their unwavering detestation of the sacrificial interpretation of the Holy Eucharist', the Counter-Reformation theologians had to emphasise this aspect of the Mass. If they failed by over-emphasis, it is fairly plain that Küng, perhaps in the hope of making reunion easier for the Protestants, fails by under-emphasis.

Reading carefully the pages in which Küng discusses the theological emphasis in the renewal of the Canon of the Mass, one is surprised to find that he makes no mention of the offering by the Church of the Body and Blood of Christ in sacrifice. The celebration of the Eucharist, he tells us 'is a powerfully effective celebration of both commemoration and thanksgiving'. The people, together with the priest, 'bring up, or present, their gifts (bread and wine), as a visible expression of their mindfulness of and gratitude to God... The presentation of these gifts (our spiritual "offering" or *sacrificium laudis* consists in the bringing up of gifts in homage – there is no question of destroying or annihilating them) is at the same time an expression of our attitude of obedience and surrender to God's will, which should correspond to the attitude of obedience and surrender of our High Priest, who made the ultimate act of submission on the Cross. The rite, indeed makes a veiled allusion to the fact that when the priest, celebrating with the people, reaches the climax of the eucharistic prayer – that is, when he says the words of consecration – he is not only, by virtue of his words and actions, the spokesman of the people in the congregation, but also actually stands in the place of the one who is present and in reality acting here – Christ himself. The offering of the Church can only be understood when it is seen as the result of Christ's complete surrender of himself. The gifts which by being offered in thanksgiving are consecrated into Christ himself, are received in the communion of the sacred meal' [1].

Here we have the people offering bread and wine, as an expression of their attitude of obedience and submission to God's will, an offering which they make as the result of Christ's complete surrender of Himself. What one would have expected to find is a clear statement that priest and people join in offering the Body and Blood of Christ as a sacrifice of thanksgiving and propitiation.

This might seem to be captious criticism were it not for the fact that Küng is so sparing in his references to the sacrificial aspect of the Mass. Take for example this description of the Holy Sacrifice: 'It (the Mass) was, of course, all down the centuries essentially the same Mass; the same thanksgiving ceremony, the same thanksgiving meal, in which we remember the great things that God has done for us in his Son Jesus Christ' [2]. This is a description of the Mass that would have been quite acceptable to Luther. Nor would he have found anything to cavil at in the statement made a few pages later that 'the Mass has always been the same ceremony of remembrance and thanksgiving, the same meal' [3].

We find similar language in his discussion of liturgical reform: 'The basic structure of the Mass is quite simple and easy to understand. It consists essentially of the prayer of thanksgiving, which incorporates the commemorative words of consecration, and the eucharistic meal' [4]. And a little later in the same work referring to the Mass as it was during the High Middle Ages: 'The original meaning of the Mass as a celebra-

1. CA. pp. 141–142.
2. WB. p. 49.
3. WB. p. 53.
4. CA. pp. 99–100.

tion in thanksgiving and in commemoration of the Last Supper is often lost' [1].

Nor is it reassuring to find in a chapter in which we are urged to meet the Protestant claims for a closer approximation of the Mass to the pattern of the Last Supper, the following passage: 'It cannot be denied that the original and inherent fundamental structure of the eucharistic element in the Mass has become overlaid and obscured by non-essentials. In its original form the Mass was a simple and universally intelligible celebration, consisting of thanksgiving and the sacred meal' [2].

Does Küng say anywhere explicitly that the Mass is not only a commemoration of the Last Supper and the sacrifice of the Cross, but also a sacrifice of the Body and Blood of Christ offered here and now to the Father? A careful examination of his works has revealed three passages in which he mentions, briefly and rather obliquely, this aspect of the Mass. He refers in one place to 'the sacrificial part of the Mass' [3], and he has two accounts of the activity of the faithful at Mass which include the word 'offering', one of these being quite clear, the other doubtful. The first reads: 'Giving thanks for, commemorating, offering up, and eating together the body of the Lord' [4] the second, less clear: 'That is why we pray and sing, praising and thanking and offering (offering what?), and that is why in thankful remembrance we eat the body of the Lord...' [5]

In several places Küng, starting from the philology of the word 'eucharistia', which means 'thanksgiving', develops the theme that Mass is a time for *thinking*

1. CA. p. 102.
2. CA. p. 112.
3. CA. p. 105.
4. CA. p. 106.
5. WB. p. 53.

and *thanking*. It is rather a pity that he did not complete the philological picture by mentioning, as Jungmann does, that 'already in Philo *eucharistia* does not only mean thanksgiving, but a sacrifice for the purpose of giving thanks', and that 'by a Christian *gratias agere* is meant an *eucharistia,* a thanksgiving which terminates sacrificially in the self-oblation of Christ' [1]. Admittedly the inclusion of such remarks as these would make his account of the Mass less ecumenical.

Liturgy

In his encyclical *Mediator Dei,* which may be described as the charter of the modern liturgical movement, Pope Pius XII defines the liturgy as 'the public worship which our Redeemer, the Head of the Church, offers to the Heavenly Father and which the community of the Church's faithful pays to its Founder and through Him to the Eternal Father; briefly, it is the whole public worship of the Mystical Body of Christ, Head and members' [2].

Since it is through their participation in the sacred liturgy that the faithful fulfil their duty of public, social worship, it is desirable that they should play an active part in the liturgical ceremonies, and one of the principal objects of the encyclical was to stimulate them to a more active participation. But it had another object also, for if the lazy and negligent needed stimulating, there were others, over-venturesome, who needed to be restrained. 'While we regret, the Pope wrote, 'that in some quarters there is little or no interest in the liturgy or understanding of it, at the same

1. *The Mass of the Roman Rite,* Abridged edn. Burns Oates, London 1959, pp. 16, 390.
2. *Christian Worship,* ECTS edn. nn. 20.

time we observe elsewhere, with anxiety and apprehension, an undue fondness for innovation and a tendency to stray from the path of truth and prudence.
Certain plans and suggestions for the liturgical revival
are mingled with principles which, either in fact or
by implication, jeopardize the sacred cause they are
intended to promote and sometimes introduce errors
concerning faith and ascetical doctrine' [1].

Among the errors which the Pope condemned were
the false antinomy between public and private prayer,
a wrong interpretation of the dictum 'lex orandi, lex
credendi', the repudiation of 'private' Masses, and
liturgical archaeologism, or 'the mania for restoring
primitive usages in the liturgy'.

On this subject of liturgical 'archaeologism' the Pope
writes: 'The liturgy of the early ages is worthy of vene-
ration; but an ancient custom is not to be considered
better, either in itself or in relation to later times and
circumstances, just because it has the flavour of antiquity. More recent liturgical rites are also worthy of
reverence and respect, because they too have been introduced under the guidance of the Holy Ghost, who
is with the Church in all ages even to the consummation of the world. These, too, are means which the
august Bride of Christ uses to stimulate and foster
the holiness of men.

'To go back in mind and heart to the sources of
the sacred liturgy is wise and praiseworthy. The study
of liturgical origins enables us to understand better
the significance of festivals and the meaning of liturgical formulas and ceremonies. But the desire to restore
everything indiscriminately to its ancient condition is
neither wise nor praiseworthy' [2].

Küng outlines the programme of what he calls 'the

1. Ibid. n. 7.
2. *Christian Worship*, ECTS, n. 65–66.

modern liturgical movement', but from his account of the proposals the movement favours, it seems that what he is talking about is the 'avant-garde', the 'venturesome spirits' mentioned in the encyclical. I doubt whether the whole liturgical movement wants to see 'private' Masses suppressed [1], especially in view of the Pope's categorical repudiation of this view. 'We have to deplore', Pope Pius XII wrote, 'certain exaggerations and travesties of the truth which do not conform to the genuine teaching of the Church. There are some who entirely disapprove of Masses that are offered privately and without a congregation, as though these were a departure from the original form of the sacrifice. Some even say that priests cannot say Mass at several altars at the same time, because this is to split up the community and jeopardize its unity. And there are others who go so far as to claim that it is necessary for the people to confirm and ratify the sacrifice in order that it may have its power and efficacy...

'On this subject we may repeat the observations of Pope Benedict XIV on the definitions of the Council of Trent: 'It is first to be noted that it cannot occur to any of the faithful to suppose that private Masses, in which only the priest receives Eucharistic Communion, are on that account deprived of their character as a perfect and complete unbloody sacrifice instituted by Christ our Lord, and consequently to be regarded as illicit. The faithful know, or if not they can easily be told, that the Council of Trent, relying on the doctrine perpetually preserved by the tradition of the Church, condemned the false opinion of Luther which contradicted it: 'If anyone say that Masses at which only the priest communicates sacramentally are illicit

1. Cf. CA. pp. 115, 120.

and therefore to be abolished, let him be anathema' [1].

Küng advocates a sweeping simplification of the liturgy as a means to reunion. It is necessary, he says, 'to go back to the very oldest of the Church's traditions' and to restore the Canon of the Mass, so that it 'conforms more closely to the model of the earliest Roman Rite', the Canon of Hippolytus. If this programme (which surely smacks of the 'archaeologism' deplored by Pope Pius XII) were carried out, it would, in Küng's opinion, prove a decisive factor in the work of reunion. He writes: 'What this Council has in mind is the renewal of the Church as a preparation for the reunion of all separated Christians, with ecclesiastical worship as the central point of this renewal. And this renewal of Christian worship in conformity to the prevalent conditions of a new age can only be good if it is derived from the Gospel of Christ, from its origins. In the Catholic Mass, what ultimately matters is simply that the Lord's command, "Do this in memory of me" is obediently carried out. Do *this,* and not this, that or the other, however beautiful, impressive or long-established it may be. But is it not true that this very thing that our Lord commanded us to do has become obscured over the centuries?' [1]

What Küng here proposes would involve the abandonment of liturgical forms developped in the course of ages and a reversion to something starkly primitive, in the hope that this may meet with the approval of our separated brethren, or at least those among them who view with grave suspicion all forms of ritual. There is to be a place in the Church for the Orthodox with their elaborate Byzantine rite, and even for the Anglicans with their stately ceremonial, but the Roman Rite must be radically revised. What the Church evolved in the centuries before St. Gregory the Great

1. CA. pp. 96–97.

may have served well enough in earlier non-ecumenical times, but we must discard it because it offends Lutheran and Calvinist susceptibilities: 'The ceremonies of solemn High Mass today have a disturbing effect upon people who prefer to aim at simplicity and straightforwardness' [1]. The others – and they are not a few – who delight in dignified and elaborate ceremonial may be ignored. Who are they to stand in the way of the movement towards reunion?

Reunion, it seems, is to be achieved, not primarily on a doctrinal basis but by the Church's adoption of a form of worship that will be palatable to extreme Evangelicals: 'If Catholic worship is successfully refashioned in a more ecumenical form, the effect on the whole movement towards reunion with our separated brethren will be decisive' [2].

Küng's view that the refashioning of the liturgy into something more acceptable to our separated brethren would have a decisive effect on the movement towards reunion seems to rest on an erroneous interpretation of the dictum *lex orandi lex credendi*, as if the liturgy were 'a sort of touchstone by which to judge which truths are to be held by faith', and anyone who was prepared to participate in our liturgical worship could be presumed to share our faith. From the nature of the case, the decisive factor in reunion must be unity in faith, achieved through the acceptance by our separated brethren of the supreme teaching authority of the Church. Unity in faith must precede unity in worship. As Pope Pius XII says, interpreting the axiom *lex orandi, lex credendi*: 'If we wanted to state quite clearly and absolutely the relation existing between the faith and the sacred liturgy, we could rightly say that "the law of our faith

1. CA. p. 101.
2. CA. pp. 110–111.

must establish the law of our prayer" ' [1]. To suggest that the liturgy can be the decisive factor in reunion is to put the cart before the horse, as our separated brethren themselves admit. 'The only unity we are concerned with', says Dr. Visser 't Hooft, 'is unity in obedience to truth' [2].

But if on the one hand Küng exaggerates the role of the liturgy in hastening the day of reunion, on the other he seems to minimize the connection between the Protestant liturgies and the Protestant faith of which they are the expression. He writes: 'Liturgical reform on these lines would make room for reunion with our separated brethren, to whom, in liturgical matters, wide liberty (in the form of a different "rite") could be allowed, within the bounds of a fundamental unity' [3].

In making this suggestion Küng is not very specific, but he seems to envisage a situation where the Church would embrace within the bounds of fundamental unity a Roman rite, a Lutheran rite, a Calvinist rite and an Anglican rite, the Roman rite having been streamlined to bring it into harmony with the legitimate demands of Lutherans, Calvinists and Anglicans. How, one asks, could Roman, Lutheran, Calvinist and Anglican rites exist within the bounds of unity, fundamental or otherwise, seeing that these Protestant liturgies are the expression of a Protestant faith in the Eucharist? It is well known, for example, that Cranmer, when drawing up the Communion service for the Book of Common Prayer issued in 1552, carefully eliminated any term that might suggest, however remotely, that the Holy Eucharist is a sacrifice [4]. Could the Church approve of

1. *Christian Worship* ECTS, n. 52.
2. Quoted by Greenstock, art. cit., p. 601.
3. CRR. p. 176.
4. Cf. Clark, *Eucharistic Sacrifice and the Reformation*.

rites which, at best, maintain a studied silence regarding the sacrificial character of the Mass. And if she insisted, as she would have to do, on the explicit acknowledgement of the Mass as a sacrifice, what is the point in allowing these groups to use a different 'rite', so essentially unlike what they have been accustomed to?

In Küng's brief account of the history of the development of the Roman Mass [1] there are several inaccuracies. Thus the Mass as St. Justin describes it in his Apology can hardly be called 'an extremely simple celebration'; the priest did *not* face the people in the Mass of the sixth century, as is clear from Ordo Romanus I; the silent Canon was *not* introduced in the High Middle Ages because the people no longer knew Latin, but came in much earlier – probably in the sixth century – and is probably due to the tendency of the priest to continue silently while the congregation were finishing the *Sanctus* [2].

Commenting on Küng's reconstruction of liturgical history. Robert J. Mullins writes: 'Küng is not responding to history. He wants a certain kind of Mass for pastoral reasons. The Mass of the second century, as he reconstructs it, corresponds to his ideal, and so he appeals to it as to his model. But what he is actually doing is constructing a liturgy' [3].

It is fairly plain that Küng chooses the Liturgy of Hippolytus as his model for ecumenical reasons. Hippolytus makes hardly any explicit reference to the sacrificial character of the Mass, so that a liturgy constructed on this pattern would be more acceptable to Lutherans and other Protestants than the present Ro-

---

1. CA. pp. 98–104.
2. Cf. Archdale King, *The Liturgy of the Roman Church,* Longmans, London 1957 Appendix VII pp. 429–432.
3. Cf. *The Sign* Nov. 1963, p. 5.

man Rite, which is so explicit on the subject of sacrifice. In harking back to antiquity Küng chooses carefully. It would never have served his purpose to propose as a model the *Euchologion* of Serapion, in which we find these words: 'Complete this sacrifice with Thy power and with Thy participation, for it is to Thee we have offered up this living sacrifice, this unbloody Gift. To Thee we have offered this Bread, the oblation of the Body of the only-begotten' [1]. But if Hippolytus, why not Serapion?

1. Cf. Jungmann op. cit. p. 23.

CHAPTER 3

True and False Ecumenism

Ecumenism, the movement of the various Christian bodies towards closer association with one another in the hope of ultimate reunion, is one of the most striking religious phenomena of our time. A number of Protestant communions, distressed by their disunity and realizing the need to join forces in a world rapidly being dechristianized, held several conferences to discuss, and where possible, to settle their differences. As a result of these there eventually came into being the World Council of Churches, of which various Orthodox groups have since become members. There has been a growing interest in Catholic circles in this tendency among non-Catholic bodies towards closer association. Theologians have attended inter-confessional conferences as observers, and the late Pope established the Secretariat for Christian Unity and invited non-Catholic observers to the Second Vatican Council.

From this closer association of non-Catholic groups with one another and with the Church much good has resulted. Misapprehensions have been removed and with them some of the items that were thought to constitute serious obstacles in the way of reunion. On the other hand, in many instances discussion has led to the clear formulation of doctrinal positions that any plainly irreconcilable, and this not only on issues where Catholic differs from Protestant but also on issues where Protestants differ among themselves, e.g. whether the Church is *iure divino* episcopal in her constitution. Thus one result of the ecumenical movement has been to destroy any easy optimism about the prospects of reunion in the near future.

This discouraging result of the ecumenical approach has not always been clearly perceived and some writers convey the impression that Catholic and Protestant are closer doctrinally than is the case. 'Some Catholic writers', Greenstock remarked, 'have not yet caught up with non-Catholics in this matter, and seem to have the impression that many of the doctrinal differences of the past have lost much of their actuality nowadays. In fact, the opposite is the truth. The ecumenical movement has brought about a re-affirmation of certain doctrinal positions in non-Catholic circles' [1].

What is true of inter-Protestant differences is true also of the differences between Catholic and Protestant; they have been underlined by ecumenical encounter, when this has been properly conducted. The rules which Catholics must follow in ecumenical encounter have been clearly formulated by the Holy Office in the following terms: 'Catholic teaching is to be set forth and explained whole and entire, and none of its truths must be passed over in silence or cloaked in ambiguity, for example, the truths concerning the nature and means of salvation, the constitution of the Church, the Roman Pontiff's primacy of jurisdiction, and the certainty that true reunion can only come from the return of dissidents to the one, true Church of Christ... All this must be stated clearly and openly, since they are seeking the truth, and real union will never be found outside the truth' [2].

True Catholic ecumenism will therefore do full justice to all the doctrines of the Church, not minimizing those which our separated brethren find it difficult to accept, and this not only out of loyalty to Catholic truth but also in charity to the non-Catholic. To lead

1. Art. cit. p. 600.
2. Cf. *The Tablet*, London, March 4, 1950.

those outside the Church to believe that reunion is possible on any other terms than complete submission to her teaching authority and unreserved acceptance of all her doctrines can only result sooner or later in disenchantment.

Küng's prescription for reunion is a very curious affair in which he does his best to have it both ways, declaring that there is to be no playing down of the truth and then denying that reunion will involve for the Protestant a return to the unity of the Church. He writes: 'How can Catholics and Protestants come together? We said before, through a renewal of the Church. But this does not only mean a Catholic reform doing justice to all that is valid in Protestant demands. It also means a Protestant reform doing justice to all that is valid in Catholic demands. It does *not* mean playing down the truth, soft-pedalling our differences, making false syntheses and easy compromises, but self-searching, self-criticism, self-reform – in the light of the Gospel of Jesus Christ, and with our separated brothers in mind. If Catholics carry out Catholic reform and Protestants carry out Protestant reform, both according to that Gospel image, then, because the Gospel is one, reunion need not remain an utopian dream. Reunion will then be neither a Protestant 'return' nor a Catholic "capitulation", but a brotherly approach from both sides, with neither consciously calculating, on the other's behalf, which of them has more steps to take; an approach penetrated through and through with love, and wholly determined by truth' [1].

An approach wholly determined by truth cannot be conducted on terms like these. For the truth is that the Catholic Church is the one, true Church, to which dissidents must return, and the Church would be false

1. CRR. p. 100.

to herself and to the dissidents if she failed to proclaim, quite unambiguously, this truth. As Leeming says in his masterly treatise on ecumenism: 'The Roman Church has a duty to her own members, to dissident fellow-Christians and to the whole world, to assert her claim of uniqueness, unity and visibility, and not to allow it to be obscured' [1].

There is no doubt at all that in Küng's programme all these distinctive characteristics of the Catholic Church are obscured. Thus he says that Protestant reform equally with Catholic reform, is a renewal of the Church, as if Catholics and Protestants were both members of the Church. Catholic and Protestant meet on equal terms since both have deviated from the Gospel. What will bring them together into a unity that will constitute a *tertium quid,* is reform carried out on one side and on the other, in the light of the Gospel of Christ. Neither will calculate, still less say, which has the further distance to go. Thus the Catholic could well admit that the Lutheran interpretation of the Gospel is closer to the mind of Christ than the Catholic. Or it may be that Küng prescinds from all interpretation of the Gospel, since 'the Gospel is but one'. If this is what he means, then the Gospel, un-interpreted by anyone, will suffice to bring all Christians into unity. This is a position which hitherto has not found much favour with Catholic theology. According to the old-style, pre-ecumenical theology, unity in faith is secured by the teaching authority of the Church, especially that of the Pope, and the Gospel by itself is notoriously ineffectual in this respect as the history of Protestantism makes plain. It appears that the newer, ecumenical theology views the matter in a different light.

1. *The Churches and the Church* by B. Leeming, S.J. (West-minster, Md.: The Newman Press, 1960), p. 240.

If it is a spurious ecumenism that allows the uniqueness of the Church to be obscured, what are we to think of those many passages in which Küng speaks of Catholic and Protestant as having 'the same common Christian tradition', 'the same common origin', a 'common faith' [1]? Take this passage for example: 'We became aware once more of our common faith. We became aware once more of everything that Catholics and Protestants have in common; the same God and Father, the same Lord Jesus Christ, the same baptism, the same word of God in the Scriptures, the same Lord's Prayer... [2] Catholic and Protestant may have the same God and Father, the same baptism, and so forth, but surely not the same faith. Otherwise, what is the meaning of the terms 'Catholic' and 'Protestant'?

There is a similar identification of what is not identical in this statement that Catholic and Protestant have the same standards: 'If Catholics and Protestants both try, while bearing each other in mind, to get closer to their own standards, then (since the standard is the same for both) they and their basic demands must more and more coincide with one another' [3]. How can the standard be the same for both, when the standard for the Catholic is the Gospel as interpreted by the Church, and the standard for the Protestant is the Gospel as interpreted by Luther, or Calvin or General Booth, or the individual Protestant himself?

The same criticism can be offered of Küng's admonition not to condemn the views of others, since they believe in the same Gospel: 'A simple condemnatory criticism is, then, since other Christians believe in the same Gospel, out of the question. Special care will be

1. CRR. pp. 111–114.
2. WB. pp. 78–79.
3. CRR. p. 100.

needed when criticising "the others", since it may often emerge, after closer examination, that they believe the very same thing in the very same way, though expressed perhaps with different words and concepts'[1]. Küng's position here is surely akin to scepticism, not to say solipsism, for if concepts can be different and the realities they signify completely identical – 'the very same thing in the very same way' – it is hard to see how one human being can communicate with another, since communication supposes an identity of concepts. If two parties in a discussion are employing words and concepts that are really different, then they are not talking about the same thing known in the very same way, but about two different things.

The claim of the Catholic Church to be the only true Church is not really parallelled in any other communion, with the possible exception of such sects as the Jehovah's Witnesses. The orthodox Church is a loose confederation of autocephalous Churches, and the major Protestant denominations claim to be no more than branches or partial embodiments of the one Church that embraces the whole of Christendom and is now unhappily divided. Küng is therefore mistaken when he writes: 'On the Catholic side, too, we shall have to rid ourselves of that illusory way of looking at the situation, in which we see only the fact that the Catholic Church is the true Church (which we Catholics firmly believe) while sedulously ignoring the fact that, whether we like it or not and whether we acknowledge it or not, there simply do exist other Christian communions making the same claim to be the true Church, that Christendom simply is, as a matter of fact, divided'[2]. The flaw in this argument

1. CRR. p. 49.
2. CA. p. 247.

of Küng's is that the claim to be 'the true Church', when made by some Protestant denomination, or even by the Orthodox Church, is not the *same* claim as is made by the Catholic Church, since the term 'the true Church' has a different meaning in each case.

There is a similar equivocation in Kung's statement that 'the Reformers affirm that the *Church* abides in truth, though they deny that every single Council, with all its statements, abides in truth' [1]. Once again, the word 'Church', as the Reformers used it, meant something quite different from what it means for the Catholic Church. To speak as if their views were almost Catholic is to compound misunderstanding with misunderstanding.

To speak in this equivocal fashion of Catholics and Protestants 'holding one faith' and the like, is false ecumenism, for it fosters the erroneous view that the Catholic and Protestant conceptions of the Christian faith are much closer than is really the case.

It is false ecumenism also to minimize the role of the Papacy in the government of the Church and to leave in the background the sacrificial character of the Mass, though Küng declares that this kind of thing was done in New Testament times [2] and presumably he holds the view that what was right and proper in New Testament times is right and proper today, the Holy Office to the contrary notwithstanding.

The folly of soft-pedalling on these contentious issues is all the clearer in that so many Protestants are coming nearer to the Catholic position on these matters. Consider the question of the Papacy. Jalland, Cullmann and others now admit most of what Catholic scholars have been saying all along about the New Testament witness to the primacy of St. Peter. Karl

1. CA. p. 197.
2. Cf. CA. pp. 170–171.

Barth, as Küng points out, 'admits that it is impossible to establish *from the Gospel* any radical objection to the concentration of the apostolic function in Peter or to the possibility of a primacy in the Church, which might even be that of Rome' [1]. Recently the Archbishop of Canterbury admitted that if Christendom is ever reunited, it will have to be under the leadership of the Holy See, and the Patriarch Athenagoras is reported as having expressed similar views. Of course neither of these prelates is prepared to admit the Papal claim to the fullness of jurisdiction but they have made a significant advance on the views of their predecessors, and while the situation calls for tact and charity in setting out the Catholic position, this is no time to be suggesting that the Pope should not be called the Head of the Church.

Similarly for the Mass. Clark has pointed out that sympathetic consideration is now being given by many of our separated brethren to the doctrine of the Eucharistic sacrifice. He mentions the German Lutherans of the *Die Sammlung* movement, the Taizé religious community in French-speaking Calvinism, an openminded study and *Eucharist Sacrifice* by the Swedish Bishop Aulen, a much-discussed article by A. Volkmann which invites Lutherans to accept what is in effect a Catholic theology of the Eucharistic action, and the views of many Anglicans [2]. He admits that we must be careful not to exaggerate the extent of this movement in the Protestant world towards the Catholic view of the Mass, but the movement is nevertheless highly significant since these groups exercise an influence in Protestant theology that is out of all

1. CRR. p. 138.
2. Art. *The Mass, Grace and Christian Unity* in *Christian Unity* (ed. K. McNamara), The Furrow Press, Maynooth, 1962, pp. 103–104.

proportion to their numbers. In the circumstances, then, we may fairly ask whether it is opportune to speak of the Mass, as Küng so often does, in language that is more Lutheran than Catholic.

Küng declares that since there is no prospect of effecting the reunion of Christendom by individual conversions, we must think in terms of corporate reunion [1]. But nowhere does he give evidence of having faced the difficulty of how to achieve corporate reunion with groups which are themselves disunited. The Orthodox Church consists of about a score of independent Churches, so that there is no leader who can speak for all, and the situation is further complicated by the rivalry between Moscow and Constantinople. However, since the doctrinal differences separating these bodies from the Catholic Church are not great, corporate reunion with one or other of them does not seem beyond the bounds of practical possibility. With the Protestant denominations the case is different. Since Protestantism is committed to the principle of private judgement, the beliefs of individuals belonging to the one Church will often differ widely. Recently the Bishop of Leeds drew attention to this difficulty in the case of the Anglicans; 'You can never be sure that the non-Catholic with whom you are speaking even if he is a bishop, believes in the Virgin Birth of Christ or His bodily resurrection from the dead' [2].

There is greater doctrinal unity among the Lutherans, the Protestants with whom Küng is most in contact, and he may think that the Lutheran Church is typical of Protestantism as a whole. But Moderism has made serious inroads even among the Lutherans, and one cannot surely infer that because a man is a

1. CRR. pp. 94–95.
2. Quoted in *The Advocate,* Melbourne, Dec. 26, 1963, p. 13.

Lutheran, he must believe in the divinity of Christ or his bodily resurrection from the dead.

Therefore, however desirable corporate reunion may be, a realistic ecumenism will recognize that, as things stand at present, it could be brought about only if one were prepared to indulge in the sophistry and equivocation so brilliantly satirized by Ronald Knox in *Reunion All Round*.

Conclusion

When one has finished writing a book, one has the impression that although one has devoted time, thought and energy to the task, there is a sense in which it is true to say that the book has written itself. As one becomes familiar with the materials, a pattern imposes itself as the only one that will suit, and sometimes one finishes with a work of a rather different genre from the one first intended.

At first I thought of providing a calm, dispassionate appraisal of Küng's thought, apportioning praise and criticism in more or less equal measure. But as I came to see more clearly the drift of his argument I became convinced that what was mainly needed was strong criticism, since the good points in his work are easily discernible and, as I see it, the principal danger is that the reader with no training in theology (and some with it) will fail to discriminate and will accept the questionable ideas as well as those that are sound.

Küng himself wields a vigorous pen and is a champion of free discussion. So he can hardly object if his ideas are roughly handled. The issues are important and I see no reason for pulling one's punches; it is enough that they be above the belt.

It has been necessary to quote a good deal, and the

reader may have found this tiresome. But this seemed the only way to forestall the objection that Küng was being credited with views he had never expressed. To the other possible objection that the passages criticised sound differently when read in their context, I would reply that sometimes a statement can be saved by its context but frequently it cannot. Moreover, I have endeavoured to weigh Küng's pronouncements in their context before offering my criticism and in one or two instances have not proceeded with a criticism which a first reading suggested.

On his showing in these three books Küng is plainly a skilful propagandist, but it is difficult to accept the statement that he is as an eminent theologian. As we have seen, his judgement has been warped, in several instances, by a highly emotional ecumenism. The Luther of his pages is almost a twentieth century ecumenical theologian unfortunate enough to be four hundred years before his time; any resemblance to the heresiarch of history is purely coincidental. According to Küng's account of the matter, the Church was co-responsible with Luther for his heresy, and Pope Adrian VI acknowledged this at the Diet of Ratisbon. (What Adrian acknowledged was that the Reformation was a punishment for sin – but Küng like J. A. Froude has a tendency to embellish his facts). He would like to see the Pope taken down a peg or two, and he regards as quite legitimate Luther's demand that the Mass be stripped of its ceremonial setting and re-shaped in the likeness of a Protestant Communion service.

It is unusual to find a Catholic theologian expressing views so novel and so provocative, and given the modern climate of opinion and modern means of communication, it is not surprising that Küng has become famous, the darling of 'liberals' and 'progressives' all over the Western world. But whether the wide dissemination of his views has helped to bring the day of reunion nearer is another matter. Almost certainly, it has had the opposite effect, for if we all, Catholics and Protestants, have the same faith, why should the Protestant bother to become a Catholic? – which is what reunion means. There is some danger, too, that among Catholics some bolder spirits may be led to anticipate events and achieve 'reunion' by going over to 'evangelical Christianity', which Küng has portrayed in so favourable a light.

The reunion of Christendom is a worthy end. But in the pursuit of worthy ends one must employ worthy means, and for the theologian this implies complete fidelity to the fullness of Catholic truth. Judged by this standard, on the evidence of his published work, Küng is found wanting. He has failed to discharge his grave responsibility as a theologian to the members of the flock of Christ and to those many others who are outside the fold.

First published in the Netherlands
Made and printed in Holland
by Drukkerij Bosch, Utrecht